THE NEW LEARNING ARCHITECT

Clive Shepherd

First published in 2011.

ISBN: 978-1-4467-6980-5

http://www.onlignment.com/newlearningarchitect

Contents

Index of learning opportunities

Formal

Non-formal

On-demand

Experiential

Introduction

Architects as we usually know them

An architect is someone who creates the plans from which others build.

An architect of buildings designs environments for living. Only rarely will they be designing an environment in which they themselves will be living. More typically they will be responding to a very specific brief that reflects very particular requirements. Before they put pen to paper, the architect simply has to know the following:

- What type of building is required – a home, an office, a factory, a school, a hospital? What functions must this building perform?

- How many people will be using this building? What activities will they be carrying out? What are these people like?

- What constraints are placed on the design of the building in terms of budget, time, quality, regulations?

The architect of buildings has a professional responsibility to their client. They are expected to be up-to-date in terms of current materials and methods, and in the latest developments within science and engineering as they relate to construction. They use this knowledge to provide their client with a building that will be safe, durable, maintainable and efficient, while meeting the requirements of the brief within the given constraints. They could be swayed by other motives – their own desire to experiment and innovate, allegiances to current fashions and philosophies, perhaps the prospect of winning an award – but if they do, they risk compromising on their duty to their client.

Meet the learning architect

A learning architect designs environments for learning. Like the architect who designs buildings, the learning architect will be responding to a specific brief:

- What is the nature of the learning requirement? What knowledge, skills and attitudes is the employer (the client) wishing to engender in the employees working within the business, division or department in question? How will this learning contribute to effective performance?

- What jobs are carried out in the target area? How many people are doing these jobs? What are these people like in terms of their demographics, prior learning, ability to learn independently, their motivation and preferences?

- Under what constraints must this learning take place? How geographically dispersed is the population? How much time and money is available? What equipment and facilities can be deployed to support the learning?

The learning architect also has a professional responsibility to their client. This requires them to be fully conversant with current thinking in terms of learning methods, acquainted with the latest learning media and up-to-date with developments in the science of learning. As none of these is intuitive and obvious, the client cannot be expected to have this expertise. And for this reason, it is neither sufficient nor excusable for the learning architect to act as order taker.

The responsibility of the learning architect is to their client. As with the architect of buildings, other motives can come into play – the desire to experiment and innovate, loyalty to the latest fads and fashions, the glamour and glitz of the awards ceremonies – but should they be tempted, they risk failing to meet the requirement within the given constraints.

'Architect' might sound like a grand title for someone other than a head of learning and development or what the Americans like to call a Chief Learning Officer, but remember that architects of buildings tackle small jobs like extensions as well as office blocks and whole housing estates. They start off working with other architects and they gain experience over time.

You don't become a learning architect by calling yourself one; you also have to behave like one. An architect of buildings does not carry the bricks or paint the walls, although they do keep a watchful eye on these activities in case their plans need to be revised or updated. They don't have to supervise every activity, but they do need to watch the numbers, so they can react if budgets and timeframes are being exceeded.

The learning architect does not need to directly facilitate learning or be present in all those situations in which learning might be taking place. However, they must know whether or not the learning that is occurring is in line with their plans and their client's requirements, and that all this is happening at an acceptable speed and cost. And because the only constant in the modern workplace is change, they must be agile enough to respond to shifting requirements, new pressures and emerging opportunities.

Learning occurs in many contexts

Most of us go to work in order to perform tasks in return for some mix of money, status, recognition and job satisfaction. We may be lucky enough to have a job that allows us also to contribute to some greater good; we may enjoy the work itself and the company of our fellow employees, customers or suppliers; we may also choose a particular job because it has the potential to satisfy our career learning objectives. Learning may or may not be the reason we go to work, but it is an inevitable consequence, whether or not the employer or employee makes a deliberate attempt to promote it.

The learning architect has to appreciate the many contexts in which learning takes place within the working environment:

Learning can be formal, in the sense that it is packaged up as a 'course', with pre-defined entry requirements, a structured curriculum and content, professional facilitation and some form of assessment. Formal learning interventions can be based on individual study or group work, they can be delivered face-to-face or online, or as some blend of all of these. They play a valuable role in ensuring that employees obtain the critical skills they need to carry out their jobs, although only a small fraction of what employees learn in their working careers can be traced back to these interventions.

Learning can be non-formal, in that, while it prepares the employee to carry out their current or future job responsibilities, it is not so formalised as to constitute a 'course'. One-to-one approaches, such as on-job instruction, coaching and mentoring constitute the majority of non-formal learning, although employers may also choose to run conferences and short workshops for groups of employees, or to provide resources, such as white papers, podcasts and videos for individual use.

Learning can be on-demand, in the sense that it occurs as an immediate response to a work-related problem, rather than in advance; it is 'just-in-time' rather than 'just-in case'. In many jobs there is now more to know than can ever be known and such a rapid turnover of knowledge that it simply makes no sense to try and 'teach' every aspect of every job up front. On-demand learning can be supported from the top-down through the provision of performance support materials and help desks, or facilitated as a bottom-up activity through search engines, forums and wikis.

Learning can be experiential. Much of what we learn at work does not occur deliberately, as we 'learn to' do something to meet a current or future need; rather it occurs as we 'learn from' our own experiences and what we observe of the experiences of others. Experiential learning can be allowed to just happen of its own accord, but the new learning architect will want to help create an environment in which it flourishes, to create the true 'learning organisation'. Employers can support experiential learning in many ways: through job enrichment and rotation, through performance appraisals and project reviews. They can also encourage employees to reflect on their experiences through techniques such as blogging.

The learning architect is a professional

When you are a professional, others seek you out for your particular expertise in a field or discipline. They will expect you to behave in accordance with the ethics of your profession, with their interests as client to the foremost.

The learning architect will be familiar with the tools of their trade, in particular the methods and media that can be used to facilitate learning. Educational and training methods are relatively timeless, even though we sometimes update the labels ('job aids' become 'performance support materials'), so Socrates would have had much the same choices available when designing his 'interventions' as we do now. However, we are constantly rethinking the methods we should use in particular situations, in the light of new thinking about the process of learning at work, continuing research into learning psychology and, more recently, huge advances in the field of neuroscience. An l&d specialist who was inducted into the profession thirty years ago would now be seriously out-of-step with current thinking if they had not engaged in continuing professional development (CPD). Keeping up-to-date is especially important when you consider that l&d has been saddled with more than its fair share of pop psychology, much of which has gone unchallenged for far too long.

Educational and training methods are important because they determine the effectiveness of an intervention. The learning architect has to understand which methods will work in which situations, or risk pouring yet more hard-earned corporate dollars down the drain. Each organisation is different and each functional area within each organisation is likely to be different too. The learning architect has to strike the right balance in each case between formal, non-formal, on-demand and experiential learning to meet the particular learning requirement for the particular target audience, and in consideration of the practical constraints and opportunities. They also have to make a judgement on how much of this design for learning needs to rely on top-down initiatives from management and how much can be managed effectively by employees themselves from the bottom-up.

The learning architect also has to be up-to-date with developments in learning media, the technologies through which learning strategies are realised. Our hypothetical l&d specialist of thirty years back would have been fully conversant with all the available media of the time, the flip charts and whiteboards, overhead projectors and video players. Unfortunately for the learning professional, learning media do not stand still like methods – we have seen an almost exponential growth in available media as computers and mobile devices interact over high-speed networks. Whichever method you intend to use in an intervention, you have many more choices when it comes to the means of delivery. Do you want to hold that discussion in a face-to-face workshop, in a live online session, through a teleconference or using a forum? If you want to share some content do you print out a booklet, stick it on a web page or record it as a podcast?

The learning architect does not have to be an expert in each new technology, just as an architect of buildings does not need to be a skilled carpenter or glazier. But they do need to know the essential characteristics and properties of each medium, the opportunities and limitations that these afford and the applications for which they are best suited. There can be no such thing as a technophobic learning architect, any more than there is an architect of buildings who hasn't come to terms with the basics of plumbing and electrics.

What it means to be a professional

To be a professional means a lot more than simply doing whatever the client wants. You wouldn't hire an interior designer only to inform them that you've already chosen all the colour schemes and furnishings; you wouldn't engage an accountant and then explain to them the way you wanted them to process your figures (unless of course you worked at Enron); you wouldn't employ a fitness trainer and then tell them what to include in your workout; and you wouldn't buy a dog and then insist on doing all the barking.

So why, then, do we continue to encounter situations in which line managers tell the guys from l&d exactly what they want in terms of learning interventions, with the expectation that they'll simply take these instructions and run. "You'd like a six-hour e-learning package to train customer service staff to sell over the telephone? A two-day workshop to teach every detail of a new company system to all employees, regardless of whether or not they will be using it? A one-hour podcast to teach manual handling skills? No problem. That's what we're here for, to meet your requirements."

Hang on a minute, you're probably thinking. This isn't an encounter between a professional and a client, it's simply order taking.

When asked to jump, a professional does not ask "how high?" They say, "Let's talk about this a little, because jumping may not be the best solution for you in this situation." And if this tactic doesn't work and the professional is told in no uncertain terms that jumping is the only acceptable option, then he or she has two choices: either they resign and get another job where their role as a professional is properly valued; or they agree to go ahead, but only after having expressed quite clearly in writing that jumping is against their best advice.

Learning and development isn't common sense; it isn't intuitive. If it was then experts wouldn't lecture at novices for hours on end; they wouldn't insist on passing on everything they know, however irrelevant, however incomprehensible. That's why we have l&d professionals, so they can explain, in terms that the lay person can clearly understand, how people acquire knowledge and develop skills, and how best to support this process. If the customer doesn't hear this advice, they will assume that the people in l&d are just the builders, not the architects; and, if no-one seems to be offering architectural services, they'll take on the task for themselves.

Time for a rethink

Everything changes and nothing changes

Plus ça change, plus c'est la même chose

At the time of writing it is 2010. Around 32 years previously (a whopping 100000 years if you think in binary), I entered the learning and development profession. It wasn't called learning and development then, of course, it was called training, but this appears to have been no more than a superficial re-branding.

In my first week as Finance Training Specialist, I attended a five-day residential classroom course at the seaside in Hove called *Techniques of Instruction*. It was run by an organisation called BACIE, now defunct. After a few preliminaries when we explored some of the pop-psychology theories about the way that people learn, we got straight down to the real action – learning how to instruct a group in a classroom setting, with the aid of a flip chart and, for the brave and more technologically-minded, some overhead projector transparencies. This course was sold on to a professional body when BACIE closed down and amazingly is still being run in almost exactly the same way today. True, it now lasts four days and PowerPoint has replaced the OHP, but essentially it's the same.

As we shall confirm in a moment, the world as it affects the learning and development profession has changed dramatically in those 32 years. But in so many organisations (and I admit there are plenty of admirable and inspiring exceptions), training carries on regardless:

- As a default option, formal training is conducted in the classroom, typically in substantial chunks (measured in days rather than hours).
- Where the classroom is completely impractical or the subject matter of the training is less interesting to the classroom trainers, the remaining formal training is conducted in the form of interactive self-study lessons (mostly computer-assisted, but sometimes with the aid of videos or workbooks).
- The rest (and that's the major part) is entrusted to Nellie, who passes on her accumulated wisdom 'on-the-job'.

Now it's possible that this strategy (assuming, of course, that it has ever been consciously thought through) is as relevant now as it was all those years ago (assuming, again, that it ever was). Change for the sake of it benefits no-one. But even the most conservative l&d professionals would admit that it is at least worth checking to see. Has the situation changed sufficiently to warrant a rethink? Could we be doing better?

In 2006, in *The Blended Learning Cookbook*, I suggested a methodology for the design of blended learning solutions. The first stage in this methodology was a situation analysis, with three elements:

- A definition of requirements, in terms of performance outcomes and learning objectives.
- An analysis of the target audience – their preferences, prior knowledge, ability to learn independently, and so on.
- A review of the practical constraints and opportunities – time, budget, skills, numbers, geographical dispersion, equipment, facilities, etc.

It occurs to me that these same three elements are as relevant when looking at the overall strategy as they are when designing a single intervention – after all, a learning and development strategy is the ultimate blended solution.

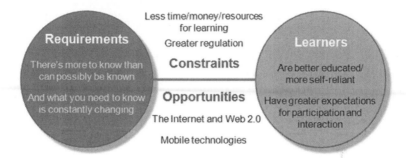

Changes impacting on learning and development strategy

Have requirements changed?

A function of living and working in what is increasingly becoming, at least in the developed world, an information society, is that there is more to know than can possibly be taught. According to Richard Saul Worman[1], "a weekday edition of the New York Times contains more information than the average person was likely to come across in a lifetime in seventeenth century England."

When the knowledge that employees need to do their jobs changes so rapidly, it becomes pointless to try and teach it all. As George Siemens[2] points out, "The connections that enable us to learn more are more important than our current state of knowing. 'Knowing where' and 'knowing who' are more important today than knowing when and how." Charles Jennings, formerly of Reuters, takes a similar view: "The word 'knowledge worker' in today's world is a misnomer. Knowledge workers actually need to hold less

---

[1] *Information Anxiety* by Richard Saul Worman, Doubleday, 1989.
[2] *Knowing Knowledge* by George Siemens, self-published, 2006.

knowledge in their heads to do their jobs than they did 20 years ago. However, they need to have the skills to be able to find the right information and knowledge, and build it into capability as efficiently as possible."

According to Robert E Kelley[3], when employees were asked whether they believed that the retention of information in their heads was important for them to do their job well, in 1986 75% agreed, while in 1997 this had reduced to 15-20%. Kelley guessed that by 2006 the figure could be as low as 8-10%.

Even in the area of skills development, l&d departments are struggling to keep up. In a large-scale survey published in 2007 by SkillSoft[4], "almost two-thirds of employees said they had been asked to carry out tasks in areas where they felt insufficiently trained or where they were lacking the necessary skills. When asked if they could do a better job if they received more training, 65.9% said yes."

I'd say that requirements are clearly changing.

Have learners changed?

What about our target audience, the learners themselves? Well, some changes are incontrovertible. First of all, the percentage of graduates in the workforce has risen enormously, as a result of the increased numbers of students now enrolled in tertiary education (UNESCO figures show a growth from 68m worldwide in 1991 to 132m in 2004). This is significant because graduates are more likely, as a result of their experiences in higher education where they have to be much more self-reliant, to have developed study skills, to be more independent as learners. Independent learners require less

---

[3] *How to be a star at work* by Robert Kelley, Three Rivers Press, 1999.
[4] *The Future of Learning*, SkillSoft, 2007

structure and less hand-holding. In some cases, you can just allow them to get on with it.

We clearly also have a more diverse workforce, with women taking up increasingly senior positions, and immigration and globalisation resulting in a melting pot of races, religions and nationalities. Coping with such a breadth of cultural expectations places a greater strain on less flexible training methods which depend for their success on homogeneity.

Over the last few years we have witnessed the dramatic effects of second generation web technology (sometimes called Web 2.0). Increasingly everyone is a teacher as well as a learner; nobody knows everything and everyone knows something. As Glen Reynolds writes:[5] "Until pretty recently, self-expression on any sizable scale was the limited province of the rich and powerful, or their clients. Only a few people could publish books, or write screenplays that might be filmed, or see their artwork or photographs widely circulated, or hear their music performed before a crowd. Now, pretty much anyone can do that. And now that more people can do that, more people are doing it, and it seems to make them happy."

Siemens[2] endorses this view: "Mass media and education have been largely designed on a one-way flow model (structure imposed by hierarchy). Hierarchies, unlike networks and ecologies, do not permit rapid adaptation to trends outside of established structure. Structure is created by a select few and imposed on the many: The newspaper publishes, we consume. The teacher instructs, we learn. The news is broadcast, we listen. Now we are entering a two-way flow model, where original sources receive feedback from end-users, we need to adjust our models to fit the changed nature of what it means to know." He goes on, "We are co-creators, not

[5] *An Army of Davids* by Glenn Reynolds, Nelson Current, 2006.

knowledge consumers. We are no longer willing to have others think for us."

And computer games have had their effect too. According to William Winn[6], the new digital natives (those brought up with technology, as opposed to the 'digital immigrants', who've had to learn later in life) "think differently from the rest of us. They develop hypertext minds. They leap around. It's as though their cognitive structures were parallel, not sequential." As Mark Prensky[7] points out, "Traditional training and schooling just doesn't engage them. It's not that they can't pay attention, they just choose not to. What today's learners really crave is interactivity – the rest basically bores them to death."

Yep, learners are changing.

Have the opportunities and constraints changed?

Let's start with the constraints and there are plenty. For a start, organisations are demanding ever faster response from the l&d department. According to Bersin & Associates (2005), "a whopping 72% of all training challenges are time critical." Some 38% of trainers surveyed in the USA by the eLearning Guild (2005) indicated that they were under significant pressure to develop e-learning more rapidly. A further 40% were under moderate pressure. The demand is felt most acutely for product training and technology training – subjects where timeliness is most critical and the content is most likely to change.

The pressure is also being felt because of increased regulatory demands. According to the Law Society of Scotland (2007): "UK employment law has moved far and fast since 1997. No other field

---

[6] William D Winn quoted by Peter Moore in Inferential Focus Briefing, September 1997.
[7] *Digital game-based learning* by Mark Prensky, McGraw-Hill, 2001.

of law has been the subject of such an ambitious, relentless and far-reaching legislative programme." To meet legal requirements and reduce the risk of costly claims for compensation, compliance training is utilising a high proportion of training capacity.

And trainers will have to meet these demands with less budget. According to the CIPD's 2009 Learning and Development Survey – which questioned 859 learning, training and development managers – annual spend per employee on training was down by about a quarter, from £300 to £220. Time will be as stretched as budgets, with flatter structures, less central bureaucracy and increased outsourcing.

Trainers aren't the only ones short of time. According to an article in Business Week quoted by Jay Cross[8], "a third of all knowledge workers clock more than 50 hours a week, 43% get less than seven hours of sleep a night, 60% rush through meals, and 25% of executives report that their communications are unmanageable." And in the SkillSoft survey[4], "40% of those surveyed said they didn't have time to do the training they needed."

At the same time, there are some wonderful opportunities, not least because of the World Wide Web. As Kevin Kelly reported back in 2005[9], "In fewer than 4000 days we have encoded half a trillion versions of our collective story and put them in front of one billion people, or one-sixth of the world's population. That remarkable achievement was not in anyone's 10-year plan. Ten years ago, anyone silly enough to trumpet the above as a vision of the near future would have been confronted by the evidence: there wasn't enough money in all the investment firms in the entire world to fund such a cornucopia. The success of the Web at this scale was

---

[8] *Informal Learning* by Jay Cross, Pfeiffer, 2006.
[9] Kevin Kelly in Wired Magazine, August 2005.

impossible." To help us take advantage of the Web, we are seeing a much improved technical infrastructure, with broadband connections increasingly available inside and outside of the firewall.

The rise in internet usage is topped only by the phenomenal growth in the use of mobile phones (there are currently some 3.5 billion users − one half of the world population) and other hand-held devices, such as games machines and portable MP3 players. As these devices continue to acquire increased power, functionality and bandwidth, the opportunities for l&d become self-evident.

A parade of bandwagons

In finding ways to meet these new challenges and take advantage of new opportunities, it sometimes seems that l&d professionals are pushed from pillar to post. They are confronted by a dazzling and never-ending parade of bandwagons, each trumpeting their over-hyped claims and each damning their predecessors as out-dated and ineffective. Here are just a few of the unnecessary face-offs we've had to endure:

- off-job v on-job learning
- the classroom v e-learning
- just-in-case v just-in-time learning
- instruction v discovery learning
- formal v informal learning

In each case, the implication is that there must be a winner and a loser; one is right and one is wrong. The falsity of this position is a fundamental cornerstone for this book. We don't want to see any more babies (some of which to be honest are actually quite grown-up by now) thrown out with the proverbial bathwater. The 21st century l&d professional needs to be able to integrate *all* these possibilities, in the right proportions to meet their learning requirements, the needs of their audiences, within their particular constraints and taking advantage of their particular opportunities. They cannot achieve this if they are swinging wildly from one extreme position to another, trying one potential panacea for a little while and then moving on to another.

Training has for too long endured the unnecessary battle between the rationalists and the romantics, the 'left brainers' and the 'right brainers'. Each camp is firmly entrenched in their positions, too busy 'sneer leading' to try and see the world from the perspective of their so-called enemy. Change will not be brought about by overcoming the enemy, nor by negotiating a ceasefire. It will come when we recognise those with differing views as the colleagues they undoubtedly are, doing their best just like you to make things work in difficult circumstances. Trainers shouldn't just preach diversity, they should practise it too.

It's time for some whole brain thinking. Less new-age voodoo. Less analysis paralysis. More learning and development.

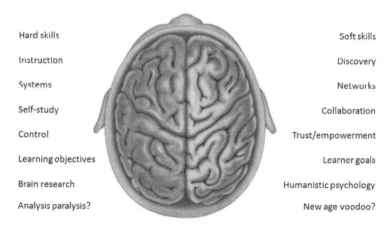

Hard skills	Soft skills
Instruction	Discovery
Systems	Networks
Self-study	Collaboration
Control	Trust/empowerment
Learning objectives	Learner goals
Brain research	Humanistic psychology
Analysis paralysis?	New age voodoo?

It's time for some whole brain thinking

Meanwhile, learners certainly have no doubt that changes are in the offing as the SkillSoft survey[4] clearly demonstrates: "Traditional classroom training doesn't have a large presence in the future according to those employees surveyed. Only 16.2% expected to be learning in a traditional classroom environment at an off-site location and only 33.4% expected classroom courses in the workplace to continue."

But there is some scepticism that this change will be brought about by the old guard of the l&d profession, the dinosaurs. There are parallels in other fields, as Max Planck suggests[10], "An important scientific innovation rarely makes its way by gradually winning over and converting its opponents. It rarely happens that Saul becomes Paul. What does happen is its opponents gradually die out and the growing generation is familiarised with the idea from the beginning."

I'm much more optimistic. It is natural for people – and that includes trainers, of any age – to resist change if this is thrust upon them. But they will engage wholeheartedly if they understand why change is necessary and if they are part of the solution. The alternative is not an attractive one, as Jack Welch points out: "When the rate of change outside exceeds the rate of change inside, the end is in sight."

---

[10] *Great Thoughts About Physics* by Max Planck, 2006, quoted in Knowing Knowledge by George Siemens.

Profile: Nick Shackleton-Jones

Throughout this book we will be taking time out to look at real-life examples of great learning architects in action. Some of these will have very well-defined responsibilities for specific populations or projects, others with a broader remit across whole corporations.

We start with a real innovator who has successfully broken free from the confines of the traditional training course and, in doing so, challenged out-dated models of learning and development.

In this profile, we will be examining two very different populations for which Nick has architected learning solutions – those responsible for production safety and all those in the BBC with a desire to contribute creatively.

Ensuring production safety

Something like 9000 employees in the BBC have a responsibility for some aspect of safety relating to the BBC's productions. As well as permanent employees, this population includes freelance, contract and temporary staff. Every one of these is obliged to complete safety training appropriate for their role.

Initially the training effort was targeted at meeting specific knowledge objectives, but Nick soon realised that what was really needed was a change in behaviour, and that this was largely driven by underlying attitudes to safety. Instead of adopting what Nick describes as a 'teacherly' approach to the training, he worked with the safety team to shift the emphasis to a less patronising, more 'grown-up' strategy in which employees are encouraged to take responsibility for their own decisions. The underlying rationale is that employees will develop, and make use of available resources, where they feel the need to do so. This is in contrast to the prevailing approach which sees employees much like blank slates.

The starting point was a colossal 13-hour self-study course which had been in place for at least a decade, originally on laserdisc and subsequently online. Nick described the course as an institution.

Assisted by senior colleagues in Safety, Nick's team set out to adopt a more collegiate, peer-to-peer tone, building a relationship with employees through an authoritative presenter with whom they were familiar in Matt Alright. Nick realised he had to think around the 'emotional geography' of the course, finding ways to hit home the points through stories and scenarios and trying to ensure that the connection with the learner was not lost at any point.

The end result was three core modules, supplemented by role-specific content. Nick soon realised that employees didn't want to listen to trainers talking to them (or a proxy reading a script); they wanted to hear from their peers – an experience that was authentic. In order to achieve this, Nick's team filmed people in different parts of the organisation, asking them what they did and how they handled safety issues in real situations, then inserting this content into an interactive panorama of the production environment. The result was a much more immersive, exploratory experience in which employees could discover how productions really work, and get a sense of what their role models genuinely thought about safety.

What the BBC team accomplished was to take an informal, peer-learning approach and fold it into a formal l&d intervention. Their current model is shifting away from courses and towards resources – pieces of content that are a few minutes long, such as a story, an interactive scenario, a short video demonstration, all backed up with a discussion forum. You look, you answer some questions, you comment on what you have seen and you see other people's comments. Each area of the BBC decides which of these resources it needs for their particular safety curriculum. Underneath this is still compliance training – a course that simply has to be done whether you like it or not – but delivered flexibly and authentically.

The BBC's architecture for safety training includes a sophisticated on-demand element. The main responsibility for delivering just-in-time support and identifying the correct training interventions lies with the local safety reps, and much of this is provided person to person. To assist in this process, the BBC has constructed an expert 'safety adviser' tool. Via a series of branching questions about what you actually do within your job, the tool suggests the most appropriate modules. A number of areas within the BBC have found this task-based approach much more flexible than one that starts with role-based competencies, because tasks regularly shift from role-to-role, rendering the competency frameworks or learning journeys out of date. By aligning the modules to tasks, this problem is avoided.

Encouraging creativity

Although there are many jobs in the BBC with specific creative responsibilities, there is a much wider population, right across the organisation, which has creative aspirations. The solution we will be reviewing here is aimed at anyone who thinks they have something creative to offer.

In developing the BBC's internal social media platform, MOO, Nick's team talked to commissioners and programme makers. Their provisional aim was something along the lines of a 'dating service', putting people who wanted ideas in front of those who had them, bypassing the conventional hierarchical process that had developed during the corporation's long history. The team recognised the importance of senior sponsorship, which they achieved with Danny Cohen, then Head of Commissioning for BBC3, now BBC1. The result was the BBC's first Creative Ideas competition – an opportunity for anyone employed by the BBC to upload a video pitch or example of their programme proposal. The value was twofold: a chance for the BBC to discover new talent and creative ideas; and an opportunity for BBC staff to demonstrate their creative potential. The latter is significant, since many BBC staff join with tremendous creative skills and energy. Danny agreed to judge the entries (including pitches from the five top entrants) and to make the best idea into a programme. Entrants were asked to submit their ideas in the form of a video, which more than 100 employees did. The winning entry, called *Wuhow*, was indeed broadcast on BBC 3.

As a platform MOO has matured, and in the process, Nick gained many insights into the use of social media in the workplace. Employees didn't necessarily want to use the facility in the way that was originally expected; they wanted a service that could be orientated around the team in which they worked, that could be used in a way that made sense to them. In retrospect, Nick realises that it was a mistake to assume that people would engage with an internal network in the same way some would outside the firewall – blogging, cross-linking to each other's resources and so on. Rather than asking employees to replicate the effort they put into their out-of-work network, the system now hooks into external channels like Facebook and Twitter directly.

The exchange of best practice does indeed take place on MOO, but this activity often needs some degree of support from the learning & development team, reflecting a shift of emphasis from courses to learning resources.

Experiential learning at the BBC

Although outside Nick's remit, he is well aware of the importance of job experience to the overall learning architecture. He described two schemes operated by the BBC Academy: *Stepping Stones* which encourages employees to take longer term assignments, and, *Hot Shoes* which offers shorter placements. The latter operates on a two-way basis: managers can advertise for employees looking for assignments in their departments, and employees can market themselves as looking for a placement. In this respect, this scheme has much more of a bottom-up feel than typical programmes designed to encourage greater job experience.

What makes for a rounded learning experience

For the most part, Nick was not required to formally evaluate his learning interventions beyond completion, but decided to conduct his own research to find out from employees what had most influenced their career and their behaviour and what resources they used on a day-to-day basis. Whilst most research grapples with the possible outcomes of specific learning interventions, Nick wanted to understand those elements of the learning process most likely to be significant from the perspective of *designing* learning interventions. The results from this survey helped him to develop the Learning Design Toolkit, which outlines key components in a truly rounded learning experience.

Nick was able to draw a number of key conclusions from his research:

- L&D departments and professionals often feel they are responsible for learning, but in reality it is learners who are the locus of control for learning activity. The emphasis therefore needs to shift from meeting learning objectives to one of building confidence and inspiring employees to learn, utilising the resources and opportunities to hand.
- Resources play a far greater role in the overall learning landscape than do courses.
- The natural process of learning is described in terms such as: inspiration and connection, challenge and confidence. Learning is hardly ever a result of a formal learning experience.
- An employee's line manager is often a major influence on an employee's career, influencing their development and their attitude towards development. A central theme was the employee's desire for a mentor-figure.
- Often what employees really want from a learning experience is not knowledge, but to build their confidence in an environment where it's safe to fail.
- You build a learning culture by building an appetite to learn. This is predominantly a bottom-up, peer-to-peer, process.

- Top-down learning interventions occupy a relatively small corner of the learning landscape, typically mandatory or compliance-related learning. This is still a vital role, however.
- Technology is helping to transform our view of learning, as it both supports and highlights the role of informal learning.

Nick Shackleton-Jones started his career as a psychology lecturer, teaching a mix of mature and immature students and publishing psychology study guides. An interest in technology and its application to learning brought Nick into the corporate world, where he has led the development of online learning strategy, content and delivery, most recently in his role as manager of online & informal learning at the BBC. In December 2010 he joined BP as Group Head of elearning. His teams have won several awards in areas including online content development, staff development strategy, innovation, and more recently for their pioneering work in the areas of rapid development and social networks for learning. Nick is a board member of the Institute for IT Training and a regular conference speaker. Nick also founded the 5000-strong 'e-learning professionals' Facebook group, blogs at aconventional.com and tweets as shackletonjones.

One more time, how do people learn?

Learning = adaptation

As human beings we must learn if we are to ensure our survival, to adapt to the ever-changing threats and opportunities with which we are confronted. As a result we are born as learning machines, capable of great achievements with or without the help of others.

Of course, we do start off with some basic, but still absolutely essential capabilities. At an instinctive, 'visceral' level, we are hard-wired to react positively to situations that, throughout our evolutionary history, have provided us with the promise of food, warmth or protection. Similarly, we are predisposed to respond negatively to those situations which have historically represented danger. These responses, positive or negative, are emotional ones, alerting the rest of the brain and sending signals to the muscles.

Beyond this rather primitive level, the brain is also capable of acquiring and then applying all sorts of skills and behaviours needed to function effectively in the world. Some of these are so important, they are set up in advance. As Norman describes[11]: "The human brain comes ready for language: the architecture of the brain, the way the different components are structured and interact, constrains the very nature of language. Moreover the learning is automatic: we may have to go to school to learn to read and write, but not to listen and speak."

Once these behaviours are firmly established through repetition, the brain is quite capable of carrying them out routinely without any conscious effort. There are literally thousands of things that all

---

[11] *Emotional Design* by Donald A Norman, Basic Books, 2004

humans can do without trying, without giving a second thought; a state that some educationalists have referred to as 'unconscious competence'.

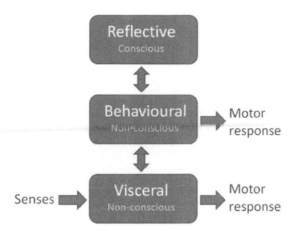

Three levels of processing (Norman, Ortony, Russell)

According to Norman, Ortony and Russell[12], psychologists at Northwestern University, the brain operates at three levels. The first two, the visceral and the behavioural, are sub-conscious, as we have seen. The third is of a higher order. It allows us to reflect on our experiences and communicate these reflections to others. And because the lower level functions look after themselves, we can do all this while we carry out all sorts of everyday behaviours, the one sense in which we can genuinely multi-task.

Just as the behavioural level of the brain can enhance and inhibit our responses at the visceral level (so we don't have to run and hide if we encounter a spider, and so we can develop a taste for bitter tasting food and drink if that's what we like), the reflective

---

[12] Ibid

level can enhance or inhibit our behaviours, so we can improve our performance or react to change. As an aside, the reflective level can also get in the way of performance, as tennis or golf players will attest when their inner voice berates them for their shortcomings and questions their ability to perform shots that have long since been assimilated into 'muscle memory'. Timothy Gallwey[13] has done very well with his *Inner Game* books, persuading players to ignore their reflective minds and 'just do it'.

Well life isn't just a game of tennis (more's the pity). We need our reflective minds to investigate, question, contemplate and generalise. That's what makes us human. That's how we grow and adapt. As Jay Cross[14] concludes, "Learning = adaptation. The strength of the human mind ... is its ability to adapt to a change in circumstances. We call this learning."

A little reflection does us good

We go to work to do things, not to learn. Depending on how we earn our living, what this doing actually entails may be little more than repeatedly drawing upon our repertoire of learned behaviours – we're literally on auto-pilot. More commonly, we're also having to work at the reflective level, to analyse problems, come up with solutions, communicate with others and make decisions. Now in the process of doing all this, our behaviours will inevitably adapt and evolve to some extent with no conscious effort on our part – we learn through simple trial and error, and by our observations of the successes and failures of others. But this is a haphazard and uncontrolled way to proceed if you value your job and your career – there's a definite risk that, regardless of the number of years that

---

[13] *The Inner Game of Tennis* by Timothy Gallwey, Jonathan Cape, 1975
[14] *Homo Zappiens*, a posting to the Informal Learning Blog, 6th June 2007

you clock up, you'll have the same year's experience over and over again.

So, at very least, we need our learning model to extend beyond doing:

Doing   Reflecting

Left to our own devices we can do quite well, thank you. But imagine how much richer our learning could become if we were able to draw upon the resources of others, who have attempted the same tasks in the past. As we look further afield for assistance, our learning model becomes correspondingly more complex:

- As we develop our network to include experts and peers, and gain access to prepared content, such as reference materials, we have the basis for just-in-time learning – learning at the point of need.

- As we extend our network to include coaches, mentors, on-job instructors and professional colleagues, and as we gain access to all manner of learning materials, we can start to get ahead of the game, to develop our knowledge and skills to meet future challenges.

- And as we build further relationships with teachers, trainers, facilitators and co-learners, we have the opportunity to formalise our learning outcomes through educational and training courses.

The people and content with whom we interact perform many useful functions:

- They **model** effective behaviour.

- They **inform** us of the facts, concepts, rules, principles, procedures and processes that underpin effective behaviour.

- They **facilitate** our learning by encouraging us to participate in thought-provoking and challenging activities, by introducing us to useful resources, and perhaps most importantly, by asking the right questions.

- They **support** and encourage us by establishing the right emotional conditions for learning and helping us out when we're in difficulty.

Which leaves us to observe, to reflect, to consume all that content which we find for ourselves or which we are pointed towards, to work with new ideas, and to generalise about what we should do in the future. Now we're motoring.

Taking a look beneath the hood

To quote Frank Felberbaum[15]: "Each adult brain is endowed with approximately 100 billion neurons (nerve cells) − half of all the nerve cells in the body − but that's just the starting point. From the moment we commence thinking, remembering, observing and learning, we are literally recreating our brains. Scientists have estimated that each of us has the capacity to make up to 10 trillion connections among our neurons, although most of us take advantage of only a small portion of this capacity. Each time we make a new connection we actually make ourselves smarter, not just because we know more, but because our brain actually works better."

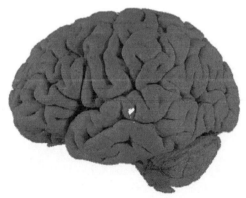

The brain − that's my second most favourite organ! Woody Allen

---

[15] *The Business of Memory* by Frank Felberbaum, Rodale, 2005

It's time for a quick tour of the brain. Rising from the top of the spinal column is the *brain stem*, the oldest part of your brain, sometimes called the 'reptilian brain'. The brain stem 'remembers' how to carry out the most basic functions necessary to keep us alive, regulating our breathing, heartbeat, sleep and waking.

Sitting on top of the brain stem is the *limbic system*, also known as the 'old mammalian brain'. Here is where our emotions reside – all those survival-oriented feelings we need to keep the species going and to recognise danger and safety (although we may also have developed more sophisticated uses for our emotions). Here, too is the part of the brain that interprets sensory data, enabling us to respond quickly to danger.

The most uniquely human portions of our brain are the *cerebellum* and the *cerebrum*. When you've learned to do something so well that it becomes automatic – such as driving a car, riding a bike, typing or operating a computer – that memory, known as *procedural memory* (or sometimes 'muscle memory') is stored in your cerebellum, which sits just behind your brain stem.

The cerebrum consists of about two-thirds of our brain, which is where our personal memories are stored. The cerebrum is divided into two hemispheres, popularly known as the 'left brain' and the 'right brain'. Although brain function is more fluid than these terms suggest, we can say generally that the left side of the brain handles logical thought, analysis, numbers and words, while the right side recognises patterns, perceives spatial relations and tends to think in images and symbols. Connecting the two hemispheres is the corpus callosum, which enables us to integrate these two modes of thinking. Research by Levy[16] at the University of Chicago confirms

---

[16] *Right brain, left brain: fact or fiction* by Jerry Levy, Psychology Today, May 1985.

that both sides of the brain are involved in nearly every human activity.

Thinking back to the three levels of brain function as described by Norman and colleagues, we can see that the visceral level can be localised to the limbic system, the behavioural level with the cerebellum and the reflective level with the two hemispheres of the cerebrum.

Felberbaum[17] describes memory as "an active, dynamic process in which old and new information, associations and complex electrical circuitry all work together to synthesise everything we know into new responses." Memory comes in a variety of forms. We've already heard about *procedural memory*, which records 'how' we do things. On the other hand, *declarative memory* (so-called because it can be articulated into words, i.e. it is conscious) is what we know about the world. It's what we have learned as a result of simply living our lives or from more formal education and training.

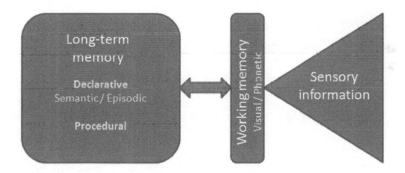

---

[17] Ibid

Declarative memory can be divided into two sub-categories: *semantic memory*, which stores meanings, understandings, factual knowledge, concepts and vocabulary; and *episodic memory*, which stores information about particular episodes or events, including the time, place and associated emotions. Episodic memory and semantic memory are related. For example, semantic memory will tell you what a horse looks and sounds like. All episodic memories concerning horses will reference this single semantic representation of a horse and, likewise, all new experiences with horses will modify your single semantic representation of a horse.

Both declarative and procedural memories are *long-term*, but quite a bit of work has to be done for these memories to be formed in the first place. The brain is bombarded with sensory information but can actively pay attention to only a very small amount. This information is transferred to 'short-term memory', which allows a person to recall information for anything from several seconds to as long as a minute without rehearsal. Its capacity is also very limited: George A. Miller[18], when working at Bell Laboratories, conducted experiments showing that the store of short term memory was 7±2 items. More recent estimates show this capacity to be rather lower, typically in the order of 4-5 items. The limitations of short-term memory are significant because they explain how easy it is to overload a learner. The management of *cognitive load* is one of the most important responsibilities of the teacher or trainer.

Baddeley and Hitch, at the University of York, proposed a model of *working memory*, which seeks to explain how we integrate short-term memory with what we already know. Their model contains a 'central executive' working with two 'slave systems', one dealing

---

[18] *The magical number seven, plus or minus two* by George A Miller, in Psychological Review, 63, 1956

with images and patterns, and the other sounds. Their work has helped to explain how it is that teachers can maximise their students' capacity to learn by combining visual imagery with the spoken voice.

For learning to take place, new information entering working memory must be integrated into pre-existing mental models or 'schemas' in long-term memory. For this to happen, those schemas must also be transferred into working memory. As a result of rehearsal and elaboration, the incoming content is transformed to result in expanded schemas stored in long-term memory.

At this point, learning has almost taken place. The process is only concluded when the new schemas are brought back into working memory when needed to complete a task. Those schemas that incorporate cues that reflect the context in which the task has got to be performed are the most likely to be easily retrieved.

If this all sounds a bit complex and rather unnecessary, then don't despair. Based on this knowledge of the brain and the research which this has spawned, cognitive scientists have been able to come up with a whole raft of practical guidelines for l&d professionals, guidelines that can be trusted and acted upon, allowing us to escape from the clutches of the quacks, the pop psychologists.

Helping others to learn

As someone who has chosen to read this book, you presumably have more than a passing interest in helping the learning process on a little, whether directly, by training or creating instructional materials, or by introducing policies that will help learners and their managers to be more effective in their own efforts. So let's take a break from looking at the process of learning to examine those practices that are likely to provide learners with the most effective support.

First of all, it is worth clarifying once and for all, that learners are not empty vessels into which you can pour whatever knowledge you would like them to have. As we have seen, learners are in the driving seat, not you. They determine what it is to which they pay attention; they decide whether or not to make the effort to transfer what they have learned into long-term memory; it is their mental models into which the new knowledge will be integrated, not yours. There is a massive difference between what is taught and what is learned. As Theodore Roszak[19] explains, "Information is not knowledge. You can mass-produce raw data and incredible quantities of facts and figures. You cannot mass-produce knowledge, which is created by individual minds, drawing on individual experience, separating the significant from the irrelevant, making value judgements."

Before you even consider delivering new information, the learner must be in the right emotional state, as Daniel Goleman[20] reminds us: "Students who are anxious, angry or depressed don't learn. People who are caught in these states do not take in information effectively or deal with it well."

And with the negative emotions removed, it is just as important to work on the positive, as Berman and Brown[21] emphasise: "It is emotion, not logic, that drives our attention, meaning-making and

---

[19] *The Cult of Information* by Theodore Roszak, University of California Press, 1994.
[20] *Emotional Intelligence* by Daniel Goleman, Bantam Books, 1995
[21] *The Power of Metaphor* by Michael Berman and David Brown, Crown House Publishing, 2000

memory. This implies the importance of eliciting curiosity, suspense, humour, excitement, joy and laughter."

Norman[22] also sees the value of excitement in learning: "The most powerful learning takes place when well-motivated students get excited by a topic and then struggle with the concepts, learning how to apply them to issues they care about. Yes, struggle: learning is an active, dynamic process and struggle is a part of it. But when students care about something the struggle is enjoyable."

He goes on: "Students learn best when motivated, when they care. They need to be emotionally involved, to be drawn to the excitement of the topic. This is why examples, diagrams, illustrations, videos and animations are so powerful. Learning need not be a dull and dreary exercise, not even learning about what are normally considered dull and dreary topics." And how can these topics be made exciting? Well, nothing works better than by making them relevant to the lives of each and every individual student.

Even the best motivated learner is restricted by the rate at which the brain can cope with new information. Fortunately there is a great deal you can do to minimise the learner's *cognitive load*, the burden on their working memory. At a relatively simplistic level you can cut back on the amount of information that learners are exposed to and are expected to acquire at any one time. More often than not, trainers and instructional designers dramatically overestimate the amount of new material that their learners will be able to assimilate. They would do better to break the content down into manageable chunks, remove all unnecessary or redundant material and focus the learner's attention on the most critical

---

[22] Ibid

material. Further progress can be made by taking advantage of the ability of working memory to process both visual and auditory information separately, utilising the benefits of self-paced learning, using diagrams to aid understanding, and supplying the learner with materials that they can refer to on-the-job.

Trainers and designers can also help the learner to *retain* what they learn, to transfer new knowledge to long-term memory. Without this help, there is a danger that much of the new information will be forgotten within hours. Dror[23] encourages setting learners more challenging tasks: "As depth of processing increases, the material will be better remembered. As the learners interact with the material in more cognitively meaningful ways, as they consolidate it with other information in their memory, they are going to remember it better. Rather than using repetition, have the learners make judgements about the material. As the judgements are more complex, depth of processing will increase."

As mentioned previously, transfer to memory is not enough; the knowledge also needs to be easily *retrievable* when the need arises. The best way to facilitate retrieval is to fashion practical exercises so they mirror the way that tasks will be carried out on-the-job. Another tactic is to provide knowledge retrieval exercises at intervals throughout the learning process. Practice, supported by specific and immediate feedback, that is managed in this way has many advantages over practice that is massed, not least because learners get the chance to detect and correct any mistakes or misunderstandings at the earliest opportunity.

It is worth reminding ourselves at this point, that the focus of this book is on learning at work, not the process of early development

---

[23] *Shall I remember?* by Itiel Dror, a paper for Learning Light, 2006

and education. As Bill Sawyer[24] explains, there is a difference: "Well before our consciousness develops into a sense of 'I', we are learning machines. We depend upon it for our survival as both individuals and as a species. But learning grows with us. Initially, learning is virtually an automatic process. Before long it begins to take on more and more characteristics of choice. There is still learning by chance or environment, but we begin to take more control over our learning."

Eventually, the principles of adult learning as defined by Malcolm Knowles[25] come into full effect. As a person matures:

- their self-concept moves from being a dependent personality to a self-directed one;
- their growing experience becomes an important resource for learning;
- their time perspective shifts from one of postponed application of knowledge to the immediacy of the task at hand;
- their motivation to learn comes from within.

Also, as adults we have a significant, long-term investment in the way we are now. Learning is a change and change is a threat to the status quo, to the time, energy and other resources you have expended to become what you are. Resisting change does not make you a Luddite or a 'difficult person'. Everybody resists some changes and this is only right and proper, because not all change is necessary or beneficial. We would be weak-minded if we simply

---

[24] *The New Hierarchy* by Bill Sawyer, a posting to The Learning Circuits Blog, May 2007.
[25] *The Adult Learner* by Malcolm Knowles, Butterworth-Heinemann, 1973

adopted every suggestion and acted on every order, however senseless.

People don't actually resist change, in fact we voluntarily and enthusiastically engage in all sorts of massive and highly risky changes throughout our lives. Changes like getting married, having kids, moving from one town or country to another, even changing careers. Clearly these are not trivial changes. It seems that what people actually resist is *being* changed, that is change that they haven't instigated for themselves.

Learning changes the brain, for good. If it doesn't, then it hasn't happened. The learner is the gatekeeper to their brain and no amount of lecturing, instructing, prescribed reading or showing of videos will make any difference if the learner is not convinced that they want their brains changed. For the gates to be opened, the learner has to recognise that they have a gap in their knowledge or skills that they believe is worth filling. And they will be much more committed to the process – and the learning will be much deeper – if they have discovered the learning for themselves. The humanist psychologist Carl Rogers once said that "nothing worth learning can be taught", which is probably going a bit far, but there's little doubt that learning by doing, conversation, reflection, discovery and inductive (non-directive) questioning will be more effective than simply telling.

Learning to learn better

According to Dror[26], "If learning is to take place, learners need to have the cognitive capacity to grasp the concepts and skills. However, no less important is the learner's ability to know and be

---

[26] *Meta-cognition and Cognitive Strategy Instruction* by Itiel Dror, a paper for Learning Light, 2007

adept in higher cognitive functions, specifically to know what they know and what they do not know (metacognition), and to know how best to learn."

Metacognitive skills are particularly important when you wish learners to be more independent in their learning, to take greater control over what they learn, when and how. They clearly cannot be effective in their independent learning if they don't know what to focus their attention on. Metacognitive skills are hard to train, but that does not prevent trainers from helping learners to gain metacognitive insights, perhaps by some sort of diagnostic pre-test, simulation or similar exercise.

Study skills are easier to address. Experience and research shows that the following activities will greatly enhance the learner's chances of success:

- **Note-taking**: The best way to make sure that new information sticks is to write it up in your own words. There is good evidence to suggest that recall improves by 20-30% when you do take notes.

- **Visualisation**: Many people find that it helps to create a mind map or some other form of diagram to help explain the relationships between the various concepts that they are studying.

- **Teaching it**: Teaching what you have learned is a wonderful way to improve your own comprehension. The very process of working out how you are going to convey something clearly and simply to others will compel you to clarify your own understanding. Scott Young[27] suggests a more topical

---

[27] *Seven little known ways to dramatically improve your learning* by Scott Young, a guest blogger at Ririan Project

way of achieving this: "If you really want to learn something, I'd suggest starting a blog and then just writing about the stuff you've learned. Whether you are studying courses or just trying to master a discipline, writing down what you know and trying to teach it to others will dramatically increase your own understanding."

- **Using it**: The familiar imperative to 'use it or lose it' is good advice. The more you practise, the better you get. As Clark, Nguyen and Sweller[28] explain: "Any task that is performed hundreds of times becomes established in long-term memory. Once automated, the skill can be performed with little or no resources from working memory. In effect, these skills are performed unconsciously." You probably know the joke about the concert goer who asks the man in the street how to get to Carnegie Hall. The man replies with a single word, "Practise."

---

[28] *Efficiency in Learning* by Ruth Clark, Frank Nguyen and John Sweller, Pfeiffer, 2006

Profile: Rob Bartlett

For this second profile, we turn to Rob Bartlett, from Farm Credit in Canada. Rob has achieved success by integrating formal and informal learning activities in pursuit of clear strategic business objectives.

Rob is Senior Consultant, Organisational Development for Farm Credit, Canada, a government-owned financial institution making loans to farmers across Canada. The company has 1500 employees based in more than 100 offices across the country, with 600 based at the head office and around 1000 customer-facing. The employees are on the whole well qualified and work routinely with computers. On the other hand, the culture of the bank is still very much one where representatives get out to see customers face-to-face as much as is possible.

In the four years that Rob has been at the bank he has seen some dramatic changes:

- A major cultural transformation stressing 100% individual accountability for impact on results and on people.
- A revamped banking system based on SAP.
- A shift in the customer base to fewer, much larger farms operating more like corporate entities and with correspondingly bigger loans.

Formal programmes

Three programmes dominate the formal schedule:

The lending essentials programme: This takes employees from day 1 to 18 months and covers all credit and customer service policies. Each new employee is supported through the programme by a team of mentors. Rob looks at each element of the programme on a highly granular basis to determine whether it should be tackled in a face-to-face class, using e-learning content or directly through mentoring.

The orientation programme: Every new employee gets the chance to travel to head office for a face-to-face orientation programme. This allows them to take a look round, meet other new hires, find out what the company is all about and hear about plans for the future.

The leadership development programme: This takes place over an 8-month period and is provided by an external contractor. The programme starts and ends with an online 360 degree analysis, involving the learner's manager, peers and direct reports. The three weeks of residential classroom training are interspersed with assignments and conference calls. The President of the company attends the last session in which they present their solution to a current work problem.

Communities of practice

Rob works closely with the company's Knowledge Management function to look for any opportunities for the two departments to collaborate. One outcome of this has been the creation of a number of voluntary communities of practice bringing together those with common interests from across the organisation. These communicate regularly using conference calls and get together face-to-face every two years. Communication between members has been enriched by the use of monthly webinars and by the collaborative tools provided by Microsoft SharePoint. Rob admits it is early days for online collaboration but that this is likely to become a core component of the scheme.

Performance support is not extensive but necessary information is available on the company's intranet. Alternatively, employees can direct questions to Knowledge Management who will endeavour to track down an expert capable of providing an answer.

Taking stock

Rob believes he is well on the way to establishing a cohesive architecture that brings together the formal and the informal, and both l&d and knowledge management. The overall learning strategy has been taken to the senior executives and is supported wholeheartedly.

Rob is keen to make sure that each intervention is deliberate and not just another case of 'putting them on a course'. Managers within the business come to him knowing that he will look at each requirement on its own merits and come up with a solution that is right for the job. No way will Rob ever be an order taker.

Rob Bartlett is the senior organizational development consultant with Farm Credit Canada. Rob was responsible for the development of the organization's overall learning strategy, and is responsible for the on-going maintenance of the strategy. Rob has a varied background in learning, including safety training, systems, sales, task procedures, cultural change and interpersonal skills. Rob continues to champion the cause of connecting learning to on-the-job performance, both in the individual events and the strategy. Rob is married with one son, and lives in Regina, Saskatchewan, Canada.

A contextual model for learning

Every context is a learning context, whether we are at work or play. We are born as learning machines and continue to learn until the day we die. We may not always be consciously learning, but learning is taking place whether we are aware of it or not, as we strive to make sense of and adapt to the circumstances in which we find ourselves.

Four contexts

Experiential	On-demand	Non-formal	Formal
Learning from (doing and reflecting)	*Learning to* (just-in-time and just enough)	*Learning to* (just-in-case / easy does it)	*Learning to* (just-in-case / all the trimmings)

In our working lives there are various contexts in which we can learn:

Experientially: Experiential learning is 'learning from' rather than 'learning to'. It occurs consciously or unconsciously as we reflect upon our successes and failures at work and those of our acquaintances.

On-demand: On-demand learning, as with the others that follow, is a form of 'learning to'. It occurs because we don't know how to perform a particular task and need immediate help to acquire the necessary knowledge. On-demand learning can be regarded as synonymous with 'just-in-time learning' or 'learning at the point of need'.

Non-formal: Non-formal learning is 'learning to' with a more relaxed timeframe. It occurs whenever we – or our employers – take deliberate steps in preparation for the tasks we will be expected to carry out in the medium to long-term future. This may cynically be referred to as 'just-in-case' learning, in contrast to learning that is 'just-in-time'. Non-formal learning takes many shapes, but stops short of those interventions which are packaged up as formal courses.

Formally: Formal learning occurs through learning events or packages with clearly set-out learning objectives, pre-defined curricula, means for assessment and the award of some qualification or certificate of completion. Unless the course is entirely self-study, there will also be a designated teacher or trainer.

Two perspectives

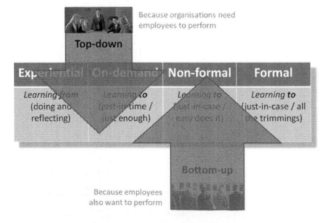

These categories are useful, but they don't distinguish between the learning that is planned for and supported by our employer, through the efforts of the l&d department and others (top-down learning), and the learning that we carry out on our own initiative, in work or outside, using resources that we find for ourselves (bottom-up learning). So, experiential, on-demand, non-formal and formal learning can originate in two ways:

Top-down learning occurs because organisations want their employees to perform effectively and efficiently and appreciate that this depends, at least in part, on them possessing the appropriate knowledge and skills. Top-down learning is designed to fulfil the employer's objectives, not the employees'.

Bottom-up learning occurs because employees also want to perform. The exact motivation may vary, from achieving job security to earning more money, gaining recognition or obtaining personal fulfilment, but the route to all these is performing well on the job, and employees know as well as their employers that this depends – again, at least in part – on them acquiring the appropriate knowledge and skills.

The need for experiential learning

Experiential learning occurs whether we want it to or not, but there are good reasons why we should be supporting and encouraging it:

- Because everyday work experience is rich with opportunities for learning.
- Because we don't always take the best advantage of these opportunities.
- Because, if something goes well, we want to repeat it.

- Because, if something goes wrong, we want to avoid it happening again.

Without experiential learning, all we are left with is the 'doing'. We repeat the same actions over and over again, never improving and constantly at risk to every new threat that appears in our environment. Experiential learning is 'doing' plus an essential additional ingredient – reflection. Without reflection, we can have many years of experience and learn less than someone who is a relative newcomer but who has learned how to learn.

The need for on-demand learning

On-demand learning is necessary because, in many jobs, it is impossible to know everything there is to know. And even if, through prolonged study and training, you were lucky enough to get to know it all, you'd soon find that most of it had changed. In the knowledge economy, it is more important to know where to look – or who to talk to – than it is to have the knowledge yourself.

According to market intelligence firm IDC, employees are, on average, losing seven hours per week searching, resolving queries and interrupting colleagues for assistance with procedures. The obvious solution, to provide some form of training, is simply not practical when the volume of information required to do your job effectively is too great or the information changes too rapidly. Formal training is arduous, disruptive and expensive and so best reserved for getting across the most critical concepts and principles, and the skills that employees use every day.

Increasingly, a better answer is to encourage learning at the point of need, when it is critical to an immediate challenge and when the employee's motivation to learn is therefore at its greatest. As Samuel Johnson once said, "Knowledge is of two kinds: we know a subject ourselves or we know where we can find information upon it."

The need for non-formal learning

More proactive approaches are needed because, however good our performance support environment, there are certain fundamental things we need to know and skills we need to have before we can make any serious attempt to function in our present jobs, or take on new responsibilities. We are, of course, recruited as much as anything, for the skills and knowledge we already possess – for our years of experience with other employers and for our qualifications. But every employer is different in terms of their culture, their particular policies and procedures, and the people that they employ. Even the most qualified new recruit requires some induction. And jobs don't remain static – responsibilities change along with new strategies, processes and systems, creating new requirements for knowledge and skill. And looking ahead, organisations and employees themselves have an obvious interest in making preparations for employees to take on greater responsibilities.

In addressing these needs, organisations can, of course, deliver formal interventions, typically packaged up as 'courses'. However, they can also call upon a wide range of more flexible, non-formal approaches, which allow for continuous learning and development.

The need for formal learning

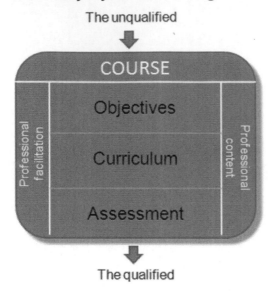

The goals of formal and non-formal learning are essentially the same – to equip employees with the fundamental knowledge and skills that they require to meet present and future job responsibilities. The difference is in the approach. The structure inherent in formal education, training and development – the objectives, the curricula, the assessment, the professional facilitation – provides advantages for employers and employees alike:

- Employers can have greater confidence that important content has been covered consistently.

- Employers can more easily track who has had what training and when.

- Employers can have greater confidence that learning objectives have actually been achieved.

- Employees can have greater confidence in the quality of the tuition they are likely to receive.

- Employees are more likely to have access to professionally-designed materials.

- Employees have the opportunity to gain a certification/qualification that will be valuable in their careers.

The need for top-down learning

As stated previously, top-down learning happens at the employer's initiative, and does so because organisations need their employees to have the right knowledge and skills if they are to perform effectively.

Whatever the attractions of a more bottom-up approach (as we shall see), some learning cannot be left to chance. Why? Because employees need basic competencies and they don't always know what they don't know, where to look for answers or who to turn to; because requirements change (new policies, products, plans), and because employees must be developed to fill future gaps.

However, it is unrealistic for all learning to be managed on a top-down basis, particularly in those organisations where change is constant and knowledge requirements hard to predict. As most top-down learning requires the direct intervention of subject experts and l&d professionals, resources are clearly going to be limited, so priorities have to be made. Top-down learning is likely to be most valuable for the 20% of knowledge that is needed 80% of the time, and for learning that is most critical in terms of risk to safety, budget or reputation.

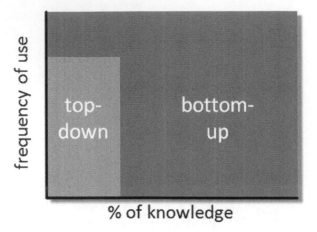

The need for bottom-up learning

Bottom-up learning is managed by employees themselves. Why? Because it is in their interests to gain whatever knowledge and skills they need to perform effectively. A bottom-up approach is needed to address the 80% of learning that is needed 20% of the time. It most needs to be encouraged in those organisations in which there is constant change and fluidity in tasks and goals.

Bottom-up learning is cheaper, more responsive, less controlling, less patronising and altogether more in tune with the times. But it is also less certain, less measurable and less suited to dependent learners who don't know what they don't know.

For bottom-up learning to thrive, employees need the motive, the means and the opportunity (just like the perps in the crime novels). They will only have the **motive** if they are rewarded for effective performance. They will only have the **means** if employers help them to develop the metacognitive skills they need to learn independently and provide, where appropriate, the right collaborative software tools. They will only have the **opportunity** if employers are able to foster a culture which encourages self-initiative and does not penalise mistakes.

L&d professionals could do worse in future than to regard bottom-up learning as the default solution, the one they choose routinely except where it is obviously unsuitable. For too long, employees have been spoon-fed their education and their training, and have failed to develop as independent learners to the extent that perhaps they should have done. Those entering the workforce in 2010 have overcome these barriers and have higher expectations. Provide them with the motive, the means and the opportunities and their capabilities are likely to astound you.

The model in action

Experiential	On-demand	Non-formal	Formal
Benchmarking	Performance	Coaching / OJT	Classroom courses
Job rotation /	support materials	Mini-workshops	Self-study e-learning
enrichment	Online books	Rapid e-learning	Outdoor learning
Project reviews	Help desks	White papers	Collaborative
Performance	Mobile learning	Podcasts	distance learning
appraisals		Webinars	Computer games &
Action learning		Internal conferences	simulations
Continuous		Online video	Blended learning
improvement			
Personal reflection	Online search	Open learning	Professional and
Reflecting with	Using forums	Communities of	postgraduate
others	Using wikis	practice	qualifications
Blogging		Continuing	Formal adult
Getting a life		professional	education
		development	

A multitude of opportunities for increasing learning exists within every context, both from the top down and bottom up. The table above shows just a sample of what is available. Some of these opportunities are certainly not new, but may not have been fully exploited in the past. Others – such as blogging, electronic performance support, online books, mobile learning, using forums and wikis, online search, podcasts and webcasts, social networking and blended learning – have resulted from relatively recent technological developments, and have certainly not yet been used to their full potential.

The model can help l&d professionals to:

- consider all the contexts in which learning can take place at work and the opportunities that exist in each of these contexts;
- assess the relative priorities that should be placed on each of the four contexts for a given population;
- provide the right balance of top-down and bottom-up learning for that population;
- create the conditions in which this strategy can succeed.

This process needs to be informed by a thorough understanding of (1) the role that each context plays in an overall l&d strategy, (2) the conditions necessary for learning to thrive from both the top-down and the bottom up, and (3) the range of opportunities that exists to support learning in each case. Much of the rest of this book is devoted to ensuring that understanding.

In the meantime you may be overwhelmed by the abundance of options at your disposal. There's no doubt that learning and development was a lot simpler when it consisted either of sitting next to Nellie or attending a class. I remember George Siemens once saying that the more choice we have, the more likely we are to choose the familiar option. If that's the case we're all doomed. We have waited a long time for the tools to arrive. Now they're here, the least we can do is try our best to put them to work.

Profile: Sebastian Graeb-Konneker

For our third profile, we take a look at how learning is architected within one of the world's largest and most successful multinational corporations. Sebastian's vision for learning covers all four of the contexts that we explored in the last chapter.

Dr Sebastian Graeb-Konneker is a Learning Adviser, Design and Development for Shell International. Sebastian was inspired in his approach to learning by Professor Betty Collis, with whom he worked at the University of Twente in the Netherlands and later in Shell. Like Betty, Sebastian is a champion of work-based learning, aided by technology. He is responsible for designing learning solutions across Shell's global workforce of more than 100,000 employees. His leaning is towards rich blends, going beyond the typical classroom plus e-learning mix to include both formal and informal elements. As Sebastian explains, "Learning happens as we speak. If you make learning look like work, then employees won't believe that it's a course they're going to."

The place for formal learning at Shell

Even though Sebastian favours informal approaches, he acknowledges there is an important place for more formal, structured learning, such as when transforming a graduate into a full working professional. He also accepts the need for compliance training such as for health and safety, although he acknowledges that this is sometimes "less about learning more about assuring that they've done it."

In his design for leadership development and technical training, Sebastian brings a wide range of non-formal and experiential approaches into the mix, including a 360 degree feedback tool and job shadowing. Where it is required that participants meet, they can do this on the phone or with LiveMeeting (a web conferencing system), as they would at other times in their work. Sebastian is a big fan of asynchronous group activities, centred around Shell's Moodle platform. As he says, "Working together far apart – that's what work is like these days."

Sebastian prefers his designs to be activity-driven, not content-driven, working back from the performance goal. The design process is global and, while highly systematic, also agile and iterative. Stakeholder management is of the upmost importance, with the learner an important voice in the process.

Learning beyond the course

Shell is really good at providing a myriad of other, less formal, ways in which employees can develop core competences, keep up-to-date with changes and prepare to take on further responsibilities. The whole approach is based on a framework of competencies. As Sebastian explains, "They expect you to be developing yourself.

And someone is always responsible for supporting your development – with coaching from your line manager and mentoring. Communities of practice have been established for more 12 years, with well-defined policies and systems.

On-demand approaches

To support on-demand learning Shell has its own wiki, with 70,000 users and more than 40,000 articles. Backing this up is a knowledge management strategy based on the simple requirement to "ask, learn, share." There is a strong incentive to share, particularly in the technical disciplines and, as a result, networking is vibrant.

As well as the wiki, collaboration is facilitated by the Shell International Global Networks, which allows employees to easily locate expertise and discuss issues using forums. This bottom-up approach has proved to be effective, although the degree of success does vary from area to area. Every employee is encouraged to establish a profile on the network.

Learning through blogging

Blogging is possible within the firewall using SharePoint, but hasn't taken off in any significant fashion. On the other hand, employees are encouraged to blog externally. A good example of this is the blog of Sebastian's colleague Hans de Zwart, Shell's Innovation Manager for Learning Technologies. Here's what Hans had to say about the ways in which the learning architecture in Shell is evolving[29]:

"The one thing that I think that Shell is innovative about is in its complete focus of alignment of learning and work. We focus more

---

[29] *What does an Innovation Manager for Learning Technologies Do?* From Hans de Zwart's *Technology as a Solution* blog – http://blog.hansdezwart.info/

and more on on-the-Job training, on learning events that are completely relevant to somebody's work. The way that learning events are designed, they always have work-related assignments to them, and most of them require supervisor involvement. You need to agree with your supervisor on what you need to do. Learning is often integrated with knowledge management – through the wiki for example."

"There's really a broad spectrum in the delivery of learning, but everything is still delivered from a course paradigm and from the idea of competence profiles. What you are starting to see is that the course paradigm is starting to crumble a bit. So it's called informal learning or on-the-job learning. I think what you will see (and we are starting to see it here in the way we are architecting our next steps in our learning landscape), is smaller, modular content pieces, a different perspective of what we consider to be a learning event. This is more of a 'pull' idea – learning when you need it, than a 'push' approach; specific learning interventions based around very current direct business problems – instead of through competencies."

Sebastian is part of the Learning & Organisational Effectiveness team in Shell Project & Technology. Analysing the organisation's business issues, he works to ensure that learning solutions are aligned to the goals of management. Following a doctoral degree, Sebastian began his learning and development career in Japan, where he co-authored some 30 TV programmes tailored for students of the Japanese Open University. Today his work includes clients as diverse as Philips, the Swiss Embassy in Indonesia, the Talented and Gifted Students Program at U.S. University of Oregon and the German National Academic Exchange Service. Key contributions for Shell include the development of the group's blended learning strategy, implementing the company's global Virtual Learning System and establishing knowledge management as a key component in learning programme designs. Sebastian is a Fulbright Alumni and founding member of the German-European Centre of Excellence at Japan's prestigious Tokyo University. He is author of five books, of which three have been co-authored, and has written over 30 articles and book reviews. He is also a certified retail salesman and has done a great deal of acting alongside his career.

Top-down learning

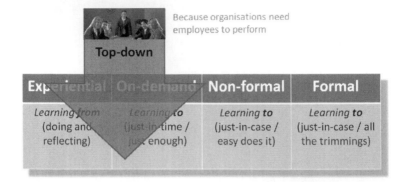

Because organisations need employees to perform

		Non-formal	Formal
Experiential	On-demand		
Learning from (doing and reflecting)	Learning to (just-in-time / just enough)	Learning to (just-in-case / easy does it)	Learning to (just-in-case / all the trimmings)

Top-down learning occurs because organisations want their employees to perform effectively and efficiently and because they appreciate that this depends, at least in part, on these employees possessing the appropriate knowledge and skills. Top-down learning is designed to fulfil the employer's objectives for improved performance, not the employees'.

The scope of top-down learning

Top-down learning occurs in all four contexts:

Experiential: Employers can initiate all sorts of programmes to maximise the opportunities for employees to learn directly from their work experience. For example, through a process of *job rotation*, employees might be moved from one position to another, perhaps from one geographical location to another, in order to obtain a more rounded perspective on the organisation's activities. Similarly, through *job enrichment*, employees may be assigned additional responsibilities which expand their opportunities to develop. Other initiatives may attempt to institutionalise the process of reflection upon which experiential learning depends – formal project reviews, benchmarking within and between organisations, action learning programmes and, of course, performance appraisal.

On-demand: Where the nature of the work that employees carry out requires that they have ready access to information at the point of need, there are again many opportunities for top-down interventions. These include the provision of performance support materials, in print form or online, at the desktop or through mobile devices; employers may offer online access to vast catalogues of books, using services such as Books 24x7; they may also make available person-to-person support using help desks and other ways to 'ask-the-expert'.

Non-formal: Of course nearly all employees will require some training to help them adjust to the organisation and to their new positions, to cope with changes and to prepare for future responsibilities. Proactive, top-down interventions include on-job training, coaching programmes and 'mini-courses' in various forms including short workshops, rapid e-learning modules, podcasts or white papers.

Formal: Top-down learning is at its most structured and controlled when it is implemented within the wrapper of a 'course', traditionally in the classroom, but nowadays just as likely online or some blend of the two. Formal learning is not necessarily rigid, authoritarian or boring – it will often include games and simulations, drama, outdoor activities and other forms of discovery learning.

Top-down learning is the traditional domain of the l&d professional, acting on authority delegated from senior management, sometimes through the human resources department (most typically when the requirement spans the whole workforce) and sometimes through the line (when the requirement is of a more technical nature). Because it exists to serve the needs of management, top-down learning must by definition be managed in this traditional, hierarchical fashion and cannot be allowed to just happen of its own accord.

To many l&d professionals, top-down learning will be their only concern and the only form of learning that they recognise or even acknowledge. But, as we know, even in the most tightly-controlled organisations, a great deal of learning also occurs on a bottom-up basis, on the initiative of employees themselves, who have their own interests in performing well in their jobs and continuing to be rewarded by their employers accordingly. As we shall see in the following chapter, bottom-up learning is more flexible, more adaptive, requires less support and in the right circumstances is capable of being highly effective. So why should organisations continue to devote resources to top-down learning and take great care to ensure that these resources are applied effectively and efficiently? This question requires some careful consideration and that is where we will start.

Why top-down learning is needed

Imagine a scenario where there were no top-down learning interventions, where there was no l&d department and no attempt at all by management to regulate and control the process of learning. Here's what might happen:

- Employees naturally organise themselves so that, when new employees join the organisation, those with more experience show them the ropes.

- Employees take the initiative themselves to take on new responsibilities or swap responsibilities with others in order to further their development.

- Employees make an effort to share their expertise and experiences with each other.

- In the absence of internal expertise, employees explore what is available externally using their own networks of contacts, resources on the internet, print publications and professional associations.

Sounds good. On the other hand, this might also be the outcome:

- Everyone is so busy that, when a new employee joins, no-one has the time to spend with them.

- Where explanations are provided, the information is so unstructured that novices find it hard to assimilate.

- New employees don't know what they don't know, so they don't ask the right questions.

- Learning is haphazard and critical information is often missed, resulting in accidents, costly mistakes and legal liabilities.

- When changes are made to policies and practices, the benefits are slow to be realised, because the changes are not properly understood.

- Employees are not provided with new challenges, so they get bored and leave.

- When expertise is not available, no-one knows what to do and managers must intervene to resolve the problem.

In simple terms, top-down learning is needed to control risk: the risk that employees won't have the basic competences needed to carry out their jobs; the risk that employees will make costly or dangerous mistakes; the risk that change programmes will fail to meet their objectives; the risk that suitable candidates will not be available when positions become vacant. These are serious risks. Either an organisation has a great deal of trust in its employees to prevent these risks becoming a reality (which may be a sound judgement in exceptional cases), or it must take preventative action itself. And that's a top-down approach.

How much learning should be top-down?

It's possible that, where there isn't that much to know and it doesn't change that often, all learning can be managed on a top-down basis. However, this is completely unrealistic for the majority of organisations in which there's far too much to know and it's changing far too quickly. So where should the priorities be placed?

On the most critical knowledge and skills: Some learning is of high importance, not necessarily because it is required that often, but because if it is not applied on the occasions when it *is* required then there could be serious consequences for the organisation. Imagine a pilot who didn't know how to land a plane in bad weather conditions, a financial trader who did not know how to respond to a market crash, a manager who did not realise the implications of firing a direct report who he happened not to like all that much. Some learning simply cannot be left to chance – it needs to be planned carefully, expertly facilitated and rigorously assessed.

On the most commonly-used knowledge and skills: Leaving aside the really critical, high stakes knowledge and skills, a judgement has to be made on how the remainder is handled. One answer is to apply the Pareto principle, also known as the 80:20 rule. This states that, in many situations in life, 80% of the effects come from 20% of the causes. In a learning context it would be reasonable to assume that 20% of all the knowledge related to a particular job will be adequate to cover 80% of tasks. The remaining 80% of the knowledge is used only occasionally. It makes sense, therefore, to concentrate resources on providing the knowledge that is most regularly needed, whether through a training intervention or the provision of performance support.

On novices: When you have little or no knowledge of a subject, you are more appreciative of a structured and supportive learning environment. Novice learners don't have the advantage of existing schemas (generalised knowledge about situations and events) in long-term memory that enable more experienced employees to cope with less structured learning experiences. Clark, Nguyen and Sweller[30] explain how carefully-designed instructional approaches "serve as schema substitutes for novice learners. Since novices don't have relevant schemas, the instruction needs to serve the role that schemas in long-term memory would serve." The implication of all this is that, if you're a skilled l&d professional, your services will be most appreciated by novices.

Where metacognitive skills are low: Those with good metacognitive skills are better equipped to learn independently. They have a good feel for what they already know, what's missing and how to go about filling the gap. They will benefit from top-down learning but they don't depend on it. For this reason, where resources are tight, efforts are more sensibly directed at those who most need the assistance. There are various ways of finding out who has the ability to learn independently. You could (1) guess based on generalisations (unskilled workers, unlikely; software

---

[30] *Efficiency in Learning: Evidence-based Guidelines to Manage Cognitive Load* by Ruth Clark, Frank Nguyen and John Sweller, Pfeiffer, 2006.

engineers, likely), (2) observe behaviour over time and come to a considered opinion, person by person, or (3) ask the people involved directly. Just make sure you don't use the term 'metacognitive skills'!

Targeting top-down learning

As we've seen, given that all l&d professionals operate within a context of limited resources, top-down learning needs to be well targeted. Determining what those targets should be is not a trivial task, particularly as many l&d departments are not that well connected to the managerial decision-making process within their organisations. The effort must be made, however, or else a high proportion of the resources expended in top-down interventions (not least the efforts and talents of committed l&d professionals) will be misdirected, if not completely wasted. As Berry Gordy, founder of Motown Records, famously remarked: "People ask me, 'where did I go wrong?' My answer is always the same: Probably at the beginning."

Top-down learning should be targeted at behaviours that are critical to the organisation. Critical behaviours can only be determined by looking at business needs.

It is nothing new to be told that training should be aligned to the needs of the business, but that doesn't mean that it 'goes without saying' or is 'common sense'. All too often, common sense is anything but common. Ask yourself how many of the training interventions in your organisation are clearly aligned to current business needs, rather than fulfilling requirements articulated sometime in the distant past, but which have no current relevance. And how many interventions have originated from the l&d department on the basis of where *they* believe the organisation should be heading, regardless of the views of senior management? No organisation ever set up an l&d department so this department could then determine the appropriate direction for the organisation. It is not up to l&d professionals to decide what is good leadership, what is good customer service or what are appropriate values for the organisation. Their job is to help senior management make their vision a reality, regardless of whether that vision is shared by the professionals that staff the l&d department.

A good question to ask is this:

What behaviours are critical to the future success of this organisation?

Let's unpick this a little. You need to know about 'behaviours' because, of all the various factors which influence the success of an organisation, only these can be affected by learning and development. You need to find out which are the 'critical' behaviours, because you don't have the resources to devote to the non-critical. And you need to focus on 'future success', because learning and development is an investment in the future and can do little to influence what happens right now. The only people who can answer this question with any authority are senior management.

The question can and should also be addressed at each of the main functional and regional departments and divisions within the organisation, as well as at various levels. For example: "What behaviours are critical to the future success of the IT department or European region"; "What middle management behaviours are critical to the future success of the organisation?"

Once you know what behaviours are required if the organisation is to succeed in the future, you need to assess the extent of the task in front of you:

To what degree are employees already exhibiting the behaviours that are critical for success?

Answering this question is no small task. If you work for a larger organisation, then ideally you'll have set up a performance management system which enables you to keep track of how individuals are performing. This will include a competency framework covering every job position; one that is up-to-date with the constant and inevitable changes in job responsibilities and which describes the behaviours that senior management are looking to encourage. In order for you to assess the extent to which these competences are evidenced in actual performance, all employees will have been regularly assessed against this framework or will have conducted some form of self-assessment. Smaller organisations may not have gone so far, but they should at very least be conducting regular performance appraisals.

If, having carried out your research, you find no gaps, then your only problem is ensuring the continued supply of employees who exhibit the desired behaviours. You should be so lucky! Chances are you'll have to ask one more question:

What influence can learning and development have on these behaviours?

Performance is influenced by a lot more than skill and knowledge, as this diagram shows:

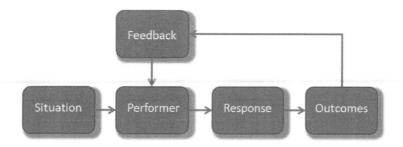

Situational influences on the performer include the clarity of roles and objectives, the suitability of the working environment, and the tools and other resources at the performer's disposal. The performer him or herself has aptitudes (indicating his or her potential to learn) and motivations, as well as their accumulated knowledge and skills. The performer's responses are also influenced by outcomes (the incentives and disincentives that are likely to result from performing in a certain way) as well as the timely availability of relevant feedback. The whole performance system has to be functioning correctly if performers are to exhibit the desired behaviours. Learning and development is only going to work if (1) unsatisfactory performance can at least partly be attributed to a lack of knowledge or skills, and (2) the employees in question have the aptitude to acquire these.

According to Stolovitch & Keeps[31], "The leading human performance authorities have all demonstrated that most performance deficiencies in the workplace are not a result of skill and knowledge gaps. Far more frequently they are due to environmental factors, such as a lack of clear expectations; insufficient and untimely feedback; lack of access to required information; inadequate tools, resources and procedures; inappropriate and even counterproductive incentives; task interference and administrative obstacles that prevent them achieving desired results."

L&d professionals may have to be assertive in conducting and communicating this sort of logical analysis. As Wick, Pollock, Jefferson and Flanagan[32] remind us, "The problem typically begins when someone in upper management decrees that the company needs to have a programme on some particular topic. And when the goal of having a programme is defined as 'having a programme', the initiative is in trouble from the start." Senior managers may be experts in determining the problems that are getting in the way of performance, but they are not experts in finding the solutions – that's your job, and this is your time to speak up.

Implementing top-down learning interventions

Having determined where the priorities lie for top-down learning interventions, attention inevitably turns to the forms that these interventions should take and the ways in which they can be most successfully delivered. All too often, l&d professionals (often on the insistence of their sponsors in the line) start with the assumption

---

[31] *Stop wasting money on training* by H Stolovich and E Keeps, from Performance eXpress, 1, June 2002.
[32] *The Six Disciplines of Breakthrough Learning* by Calhoun Wick, Roy Pollock, Andrew Jefferson and Richard Flanagan, Pfeiffer, 2006.

that some sort of formalised course is required, whether classroom, online or a blend. But as we have seen, there are four contexts in which top-down learning could occur. Who is to say that an action learning programme, a performance support system or a programme of coaching would not do the job better or more efficiently?

The chances that an intervention will be successful are influenced by the involvement of key stakeholders in the process of design, development and implementation, as Wick, Pollock, Jefferson and Flanagan report[33]: "We continue to be surprised by the number of major programmes, in otherwise well-managed companies, that are developed entirely within the human resource or training organisation and go forward with little or no input from line leaders. Their perspective on the business is different from that of line leaders; they have less hands-on experience managing hard business metrics. If they consult only among themselves, they may design a programme with strong learning objectives but only weak links to key business measures."

There is another strong reason for involving those who will be affected by the intervention and that is to gain their commitment. *Learning is change.* At the personal level, this is true because learning changes the brain – if it doesn't, no learning has taken place. At an organisational level, it is true because learning changes the way we behave and consequently how the organisation performs. As we have already discussed, people don't automatically resist change; in fact we voluntarily undertake substantial and disruptive changes in our own lives. As Peter de Jager[34] explains, "We don't resist change, we resist *being* changed." At very least,

---

[33] Ibid
[34] *A pocketful of change* by Peter de Jager, de Jager and Company, 2007

those being asked to change should be told why. Better still, they should participate in determining how.

Establishing the chain of evidence

The process is not complete, as we are constantly reminded, until we have evaluated the results. First of all it's important that we know what the reactions of learners has been to our efforts – not because this is the key indicator of success, but because this feedback enables us to continuously improve what we deliver. We do need to know whether the intervention has resulted in the desired change in knowledge and skills and whether that change has manifested itself in the way that learners behave on the job. But most importantly, we need to know whether the organisation is receiving any tangible benefit from these changes. Kirkpatrick[35] calls this a 'return on expectations (ROE)'. What did the organisation expect when they sanctioned this intervention? Have these expectations been met? It is not necessary to provide incontrovertible proof, based on controlled scientific studies. It is necessary, however, to be able to provide a *chain of evidence*: we know the intervention was well-received and that participants learned what we wanted them to learn; we know they applied this back on the job and we have seen an improvement in those areas of the business that we were looking to address. That's as much proof as most managers will ever require.

---

[35] *Evaluating Training Programs* by Donald Kirkpatrick, Berrett-Koehler, 2006.

On the other hand, evaluation studies don't always capture the true value of learning interventions. As Stephen Downes[36] reminds us: "Measuring learning is still like measuring friendship. You can count friends, or you can count on friends, but not, it seems, both."

Conditions for success

To summarise, these are the conditions for success with top-down learning:

- Top-down learning interventions are aligned with the business goals of the organisation and measured in terms of the contribution they make to these goals.

- These interventions are designed to meet genuine learning and development needs.

- These interventions are focused on critical and widely used knowledge and skills, and on the needs of novices and those with low metacognitive skills.

- The most resources are allocated to the interventions that deliver the most value to the organisation.

- Senior management is actively involved in determining needs and genuinely committed to helping make learning interventions a success.

- All key stakeholders, including potential learners, are involved in the process of designing and developing the interventions.

- All four contexts (experiential, on-demand, non-formal, formal) are considered in designing the most appropriate form for the interventions.

---

[36] *ROI and Metrics in eLearning*, a posting on *Stephen's Web* by Stephen Downes, 16th October 2007.

Profile: Dick Moore

In this fourth profile we look at the work of a learning architect working within what is very much a top-down learning environment and on a very large scale. Dick's work at learndirect helped to ensure 2.8 million people across the UK were able to make a start on their learning journey.

Delivering the UK's largest online learning service

Dick Moore was Director of Technology at learndirect over nine years. Operated by Ufi Ltd, learndirect's mission is to transform skills, productivity and individual lives by providing the best of online learning. As an adult learning provider delivering widespread access to online training, learndirect has become one of the leading contributors to the UK government's skills agenda. Since 2000 it has used technology to enable more than 2.8 million adults to gain the skills they, their employers and the economy need, helping them on their way into further training or employment.

Over Dick's nine years at learndirect, he had to completely re-engineer the offer. With 500K enrolments per year, a significant number of whom have a relatively low educational level, Dick had the task of developing a technological architecture that was not just functional, but scalable, reliable and capable of providing a positive user experience.

In addition to rebuilding the learning platform Dick was asked to reduce his budget by 50% and to deliver twice as many releases per year. Dick achieved this by bringing much of the work in-house (insourcing) and creating a user panel involving all key stakeholders. They consulted and listened to the advice of usability experts, and employed an agile approach which involved a great deal of prototyping. Dick believes that involving users throughout the systems design rather than just at the end during testing is advice that is often given but seldom taken.

The basis of learndirect's offer

At the core of learndirect's provision is a 'supportive triangle' which includes the learning content itself, the system and the support staff at the 1000s of learning centres where many students take the first steps back onto a new learning journey. Many of the courses provided by learndirect lead to National Vocational Qualifications (NVQs), which require evidence rather than test-based assessment. The system, therefore, has to accommodate the storage and management of hundreds of thousands of pieces of evidence stored as an 'e-portfolio'.

The learndirect offer is essentially one of formal learning with assessment, with an emphasis on vocational and skills-based training leading to nationally-recognised qualifications. While formal, the process is essentially bottom-up, in that the courses are typically chosen by learners ('pulled') rather than imposed by employers ('pushed').

The measure of learndirect's success is the unit cost per enrolled, completed and successful student. Retention is key, so a high emphasis is placed within learning centres on ensuring that customers (learners) have appropriate threshold skills. Students are assessed to see whether they really have the time and the motivation to complete a course. This is particularly important because the courses are low cost to the learner and therefore not always highly valued. Another technique is to use entry-level taster courses, which give local tutors on the ground a chance to check out a student's propensity to learn.

Once students are enrolled the next priority is to keep them on track. With no formal teacher to engage students, the content and the system have to deliver the learning experience supported often by learning centre staff and on-line tutors. Importantly, learners need a way to chart their own progress across time and tutors need to be able to keep an eye on this as well.

Dick was particularly concerned that the system was all very simple and accessible: "Learning is not always fun; however it is rewarding, like the gym. When you're learning, you're trying to rearrange your mental model. And with assessments to complete as well, there's going to be an element of fear. In a situation like this, you need to avoid all extraneous noise."

The system was re-designed so that the interface persisted while the student was working with content, so they could send messages at any point. And because a typical learning episode was a whole morning or afternoon, it was absolutely critical that the student didn't lose their work through a connection problem. Any incident of this sort would be remembered by the student for a long time and would cause them to lose confidence in both the system and often in themselves.

Harnessing informal learning

There was an assumption that students would jump at the chance to use chat rooms and forums, however without active support and guidance such chat rooms were often 'like the Marie Celeste'. Dick believes that they would have been more successful if tightly integrated with individual courses, but as optional extras they didn't work. Whereas, these sorts of communication technologies can be highly successful in tutor-driven courses that are delivered in cohorts, for learndirect students the informal learning element came in the learning centre or at home, person-to-person. In Dick's view "it is almost an oxymoron to try and control informal learning."

Still, customer satisfaction was 94% and has since improved beyond that. This rating reflects students satisfaction with their experience and he believes also reflects an increase in students' self-esteem. As Dick explains, "If you can give people an experience that makes them feel good about themselves, they'll feel good about you!"

Providing tutor support

An important element of the learndirect experience is that students know they have a tutor and someone to ask for help. Tutors have their own interface to the system, organised according to their workflow. This requires them to validate student outcomes by looking at scores, reviewing any free text responses and messages, and then writing a note to the student. As this process became regulated by the system, it improved retention and success. Before, this was largely dependent on a particular tutor.

The tutors received online training in using the new system, primarily with the aid of short screencasts which allowed them to watch and practise at the same time. The screencasts also constituted a valuable on-demand learning resource. Again Dick placed a high emphasis on simplicity: "It seems the glossier something is the more we tune out. Perhaps we are conditioned by adverts."

What learndirect has achieved

Dick's success in creating a scalable and highly accessible learning platform can be demonstrated by some of the numbers:

- 8,200 people log on and learn with learndirect every day;
- more than 2.8 million learners have taken a learndirect course;
- 90 per cent of learndirect learners are qualified below level two or are assessed as having a basic skills need;
- 433,000 Skills for Life test passes have been achieved with learndirect;
- Altogether, more than 467,000 online tests in literacy and numeracy have been taken with learndirect;
- 23,396 people have achieved an NVQ through learndirect;
- learndirect has worked with over 5,000 businesses through Train to Gain, resulting in more than 10,000 qualifications;
- learner satisfaction with learndirect currently stands at 96%.

Technology should be architected to deliver a service not a solution, having the audience at the centre of your design and architecture and ensuring that your systems are instrumented such that you have a measure of the client satisfaction rather than relying on 'happy sheets', completed by those for whom the experience was a success, is an architectural imperative.

Dick Moore has worked as an educational technologist for 30 years and now runs his own company Moore Answers Ltd, an IT interim/consultancy and change management house that is particularly keen on charities, education systems and infrastructure. Dick was until May 2010 Director of Technology at learndirect, one of the largest e-learning organisations in the world with some 3 million learners on the system and delivering 500,000 enrolments annually.

Previously Dick was Vice-President for Systems and Information at a Los Angeles-based dot.com company thedock.com, an industrial auction site, and before that was Director of ICT at both Sheffield College and Doncaster College, two of Europe's largest Further Education institutions. During the 80s, he was Director of a new media company Interactive Media Resources, working with interactive video and educational software, where he wrote educational software and simulations for The Stock Exchange, Shell and Tandy Corporation, amongst others.

Dick has a BSc in Botany, specialising in Taxonomy, and is a trustee of the Association for Learning Technology and chair of their publications committee.

Bottom-up learning

Experiential	On-demand	Non-formal	Formal
Learning from (doing and reflecting)	*Learning to* (just-in-time / just enough)	*Learning to* (just-in-case / easy does it)	*Learning to* (just-in-case / all the trimmings)

Bottom-up

Because employees
also want to perform

Bottom-up learning occurs because employees want to be able to perform effectively in their jobs. The exact motivation may vary, from achieving job security to earning more money, gaining recognition or obtaining personal fulfilment, but the route to all these is performing well on the job, and employees know as well as their employers that this depends – to some extent at least – on their acquiring the appropriate knowledge and skills.

The scope of bottom-up learning

Bottom-up learning occurs in each of the four contexts that we have described previously:

Experiential: Experiential learning is essentially reflective – 'learning from' rather than 'learning to'. This process can be initiated by the individual without any deliberate action on the behalf of the employer. At its simplest, this might mean no more than sitting back and thinking over events that have occurred, whether these events directly involved the individual or whether they were merely observed. If an event had a negative outcome, the question needs to be asked 'why did this happen?' Could the outcome be avoided in future or mitigated in some way. If the outcome was positive, it is just as important to know why. Why can be done to replicate this successful outcome, or to exploit it if it occurs again? The process of reflection becomes interactive when it takes the form of a discussion – talking things over. And it becomes more disciplined when it is made explicit through blogging. Employees can also choose to expand the opportunities they have for learning experiences by ensuring they maintain a healthy work-life balance. Out-of-work activities such as hobbies, travel and voluntary work will often have parallels at work. By maximising the scope for new sensory input, individuals increase the chance that they'll build valuable skills and insights that they can apply in their jobs.

On-demand: When it comes to just-in-time learning, employees have always needed to rely to some extent on their own endeavours. It is highly unlikely that any employer will be able to predict every item of information that every employee is going to need in every situation, and make that available in the form of some sort of job aid or resource. At simplest, when they're stuck, employees simply consult an expert, typically the person sitting next to them. Ideally this process will be formalised through some kind of online 'find an expert' solution, a sort of corporate Yellow Pages. Increasingly online tools are being made available to support and encourage bottom-up learning at the point of need, notably forums to which questions can be posted, and wikis which can be used to collect together useful reference information.

Non-formal: There's a number of ways in which employees can set about equipping themselves with the knowledge and skills they need to develop in their roles, without enrolling on formal courses. While each of these methods relies on the employee to initiate the activity, they all tend to require some help from the employer, whether that's by establishing the appropriate infrastructure or by committing to policies which make opportunities accessible. Some examples include open learning, where the employee takes advantage of learning resources, such as short self-study courses, which the employer makes available for access on demand; social networking software, which allows the learner to establish contacts with others within the organisation who have similar needs; attending external conferences; and enjoying the services provided by professional associations and other external membership bodies.

Formal: You would think that formal courses were an exclusively top-down initiative, but there are plenty of ways in which employees can take the initiative themselves. Perhaps the most obvious examples are postgraduate courses, such as Masters Degrees, and qualifications offered by professional bodies. There are, of course, other less formidable options, such as adult education courses offered by local colleges.

People have many and wide-ranging needs, whether that's at the level of survival (security, shelter, food, reproduction, etc.), needs of a more social nature (belonging, friendship, recognition) or of a higher order (stimulation, advancement, personal fulfilment, etc.). Directly or indirectly, learning can help an individual to meet many of these needs. To the extent that this learning is reflected in better performance at work, then the organisation has as much to gain as the individual.

While the l&d professional may not determine the 'content' of the learning that takes place on a bottom-up basis, they certainly have a role to play in determining the 'process'. Because it is impractical to meet all learning requirements top-down, it is in the interests of the organisation to encourage relevant, work-related, bottom-up learning. Some of this will happen anyway, regardless of what the l&d department puts in place, but much depends on the right policies and infrastructure being put in place.

Where l&d professionals must be careful, is not being over-prescriptive about the ways in which bottom-up learning occurs. As John Seely Brown and Paul Duquid point out[37]: "The solution to unpredictable demand is systems that are geared to respond to pull from the market and from audiences; built on loosely-coupled modules rather than tightly integrated programmes; people-centric rather than resource or information-centric. There needs to be a willingness to let solutions emerge organically rather than trying to engineer them in advance."

Why bottom-up learning is needed

Imagine a scenario in which no bottom-up learning took place, in which all learning was regulated and controlled by management, and in which the l&d department invariably took the lead. Here's what might happen:

- The l&d department knows exactly what knowledge and skills are required for each job position and are kept completely up-to-date about any changes to jobs and requirements.

- Regular performance appraisals and other forms of assessment mean that line management are fully aware of any knowledge and skill gaps, and keep the l&d department fully informed about these.

---

[37] *The Social Life of Information* by John Seely Brown and Paul Duquid, Harvard Business School Press, 2002.

- The l&d department is resourced to provide solutions to meet all known knowledge and skills gaps, using carefully-planned, top-down interventions.

- Employees do not need to worry about the knowledge and skills they need to meet current or future requirements because their employer is in complete command of the situation.

Sounds like it's all under control. On the other hand, this might also be the outcome:

- The information held by the l&d department regarding jobs and skills is too out-of-date to be of any use.

- The l&d department does not have the resources to respond to anything except the most generic of needs.

- When important changes are made to systems, processes and policies, the l&d department takes too long to develop top-down interventions to support the changes.

- Knowledge requirements change so quickly that it is impossible for training programmes and job aids to be kept up-to-date.

- There is such a diversity of jobs in the organisation that there is insufficient critical mass to justify the design and delivery of any formal interventions.

- Expensive top-down interventions are delivered when employees are perfectly capable of meeting any needs for themselves informally.

While top-down learning is needed to control risk, bottom-up learning is needed to provide responsiveness. Few organisations have the luxury of being in complete control of all aspects of the training cycle – even if it was possible to attain this position, it would probably not be cost-effective. Bottom-up learning fills the gaps by providing a response to urgent situations and by meeting the needs of minorities. It's quick, it's flexible, it's empowering. That's why bottom-up learning plays a valuable role in any learning and development strategy.

How much learning should be bottom-up?

It is conceivable that an organisation could manage without any top-down learning interventions at all, relying on employees who were independent learners, good communicators, willing to share their expertise and keen to support each other. More realistically, an organisation will need to make a judgement about how much will be top-down and how much bottom-up, based on a wide range of factors that will differ enormously both between organisations and within them. Here are some guidelines for identifying the situations in which bottom-up learning will be most appropriate:

Where there is constant change and fluidity in tasks and goals: Some organisations are lucky enough to enjoy relatively stable policies, procedures and systems; for many others, particularly those which employ a large number of knowledge workers, the opposite is true – everything seems in a constant state of flux. In this situation, it is almost impossible to create top-down interventions fast enough to satisfy the need; you simply must depend on bottom-up processes to fill the gap.

For knowledge and skills that are used infrequently: If we apply the Pareto principle, then it is realistic to assume that 20% of all the knowledge related to a particular job will be adequate to cover 80% of the tasks. The remaining 80% of knowledge is used only occasionally and can probably therefore be handled using more informal, bottom-up methods, including the use of forums, wikis and similar tools. Some care needs to be taken that, within the less-commonly used knowledge and skills, there are none which are nevertheless critical. A good example would be emergency procedures – these should certainly not be left to chance and should therefore be tackled through a formal, top-down intervention.

When expertise is widely distributed: It is hard to place too much emphasis on bottom-up processes when expertise is centred around a small number of key individuals – these people would be simply overwhelmed by the never-ending requests for help that they would inevitably receive. In these situations, it makes more sense to capture this expertise using more structured, top-down methods. On the other hand, there are many situations in which it is true to say that 'nobody knows everything and everybody knows something'. Where expertise is widely distributed, bottom-up methods are much more likely to thrive.

Where there are fewer people who need the learning: With scarce resources, l&d departments must focus on those needs which are highly critical or which impact on large numbers of people. There are simply not enough hours in the day to create top-down programmes for every small group that has a shared need. Here again, bottom-up methods fill the gap and ensure that needs don't go unmet.

Where the employees are more experienced: Experienced employees have the advantage of generalised knowledge about situations and events stored in long-term memory, which make it very much easier for them to absorb new information. Whereas novices benefit from more structured learning experiences, in which they are led step-by-step through new information with the aid of an expert facilitator, more experienced employees can be given much more latitude to help themselves.

Training's long tail

The phrase The Long Tail was first coined by Chris Anderson[38] in 2004 to describe the niche strategy of businesses, such as Amazon.com, which sells a large number of unique items in relatively small quantities. Whereas high-street bookshops are forced, by lack of shelf space, to concentrate on the most popular books, shown in the chart below in blue, retailers selling online can afford to service the minority interests shown below in orange. Interestingly, the volume of the minority titles exceeds that of the most popular, yet before the advent of online retailing, these needs would have been very hard to service.

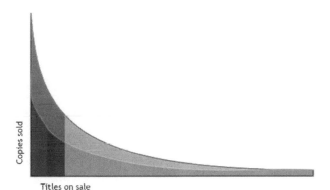

The concept of The Long Tail fits well with the argument for bottom-up learning. Top-down efforts can only seek to address the most common (or, as we have seen, sometimes the most critical) of needs. It is simply not possible, given available resources, for l&d

---

[38] *The Long Tail* by Chris Anderson, Wired, October 2004.

professionals to design and deliver an appropriate solution to satisfy every learning requirement in their organisations. Instead, when it comes to corporate learning and development, it is bottom-up learning that must address training's long tail.

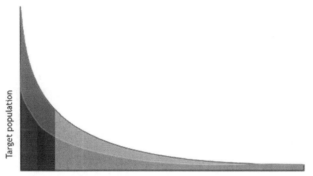

Training needs

In the end it comes down to priorities – putting the effort in where the reward is going to be greatest. At risk of over-simplifying the issues involved, you could argue that the prioritisation process could be extended across all eight cells of our model, with the most generic and critical needs met top-down, through formalised courses. Less common/critical needs would be met by less structured proactive methods; if not, then at the point of need; if not, then through a process of structured reflection. As we extend into The Long Tail, bottom-up approaches come to the fore, starting with formal external programmes and continuing across the four contexts:

Experiential	On-demand	Non-formal	Formal
4	3	2	1
8	7	6	5

Tony Karrer[39] argued that: "To play in The Long Tail, corporate learning functions will need to:

- find approaches that have dramatically lower production costs, near zero;

- look for opportunities to get out of the publisher, distributor role such as becoming an aggregator;

- focus on knowledge worker learning skills;

- help knowledge workers rethink what information they consume, how and why;

- focus on maximising the "return of attention" for knowledge workers rather than common measures today such as cost per learner hour."

---

[39] *Corporate Learning Long Tail and Attention Crisis* by Tony Karrer, eLearning Technology blog, February 19, 2008.

First they need the means

Bottom-up learning will happen to some extent regardless of the efforts put in by the employer to smooth the process. It's natural for an employee to take the initiative if they don't know how to complete a task, because they want to do a good job. It will surely be the exception rather than the rule for someone to simply sit down, fold their arms and wait to be told. However, it's the role of managers – and the l&d specialists who support them – to do more than just leave things to chance. Bottom-up learning can be positively encouraged, by ensuring employees have the **means**, the **opportunity** and the **motive** to contribute to each other's learning.

Let's start with the **means** and in particular the software tools that can provide the infrastructure to support bottom-up learning:

Blogs provide employees with the ability to reflect on their work experiences and to share those reflections with others who have similar work interests. Where an employee has many peers within the organisation, the blogging software can be made available inside the firewall, which has the added benefit of keeping the content away from the prying eyes of competitors. Where an employee works as a specialist and has few internal peers, they may be encouraged to blog on the World Wide Web where they can benefit from the expertise of similar specialists around the world. Assuming they are not critical of the employer – and you would need a policy to cover this – an external blog may even have a positive PR benefit for the organisation, demonstrating thought leadership in a particular discipline.

Search engines are an essential component in any bottom-up learning infrastructure. We all know the power of Google to help us hunt down information and, for any organisation which has an intranet or a substantial collection of online documents, a similarly powerful search facility behind the firewall is essential.

Yellow pages or their software equivalent, allow employees to seek out experts who may be able to help them solve a current problem. If you don't have the software to do this in a structured fashion, you can always provide a simple list of who to call for what type of information, on the intranet or in hard copy on a notice board. Once an employee has identified the right expert to contact, they need the right communications medium to put forward their question, whether that's the telephone, email, instant messaging, web conferencing, SMS messaging or some other format. With this proliferation of communication media, organisations might consider issuing some guidelines to help employees choose the right medium for each particular situation.

Forums (or message boards or bulletin boards, as they are sometimes called) provide a simple way for employees to post questions online, with the hope that somewhere in the community another employee will be able to provide a helpful response. Where forums can let you down is when you are depending on other users to visit the forum site in order to see the latest questions. Some element of 'push' is required to alert users to new questions, whether that's email notifications, RSS feeds or lists of recent postings that appear on the intranet home page.

Wikis provide a way for employees to collaborate in creating content that can be of use to the whole community. Although subject experts and l&d professionals may prime a wiki with content, the ability of all employees to make contributions based on their own particular experiences, makes a wiki much more than a simple reference manual.

Learning management systems (LMSs) can help employees to find e-learning content that is available for open access on an 'as needs' basis. It's important to keep the barriers between the employee and the content to a minimum. Ideally employees should not have to log in separately to the LMS; the available content should be sensibly categorised; the content should be tagged so it can be easily found using the LMS's own search facilities; the registration/sign-up process should be minimal; and employees should be allowed to rate content, so the most popular and useful content is clearly visible.

Social networking is usually seen as an out-of-work activity, where people use software such as Facebook, MySpace or Bebo to maintain their network of contacts for purely social reasons. However, in just a few years, social networking has grown so quickly, and exerted such a powerful influence on its users that many organisations are now looking for ways to achieve similar benefits inside the firewall. An organisation's own social network could be used to allow employees to connect with others who have similar needs and interests, to find sources of expertise, to form communities of practice and to keep up-to-date on developments in their particular fields.

Of course, tools are not enough in themselves; employees also need the skills to use them. Although many of the tools listed above are extremely easy to use and many employees will be familiar with their use outside work, there is room here for top-down initiatives to ensure all employees know which tool to use in which circumstance and have the confidence to become active users.

In his 'How to save the world' blog, Dave Pollard[40] lists a number of ways in which organisations can achieve quick wins with bottom-up knowledge management initiatives, by skilling up employees to make better use of the tools at their disposal:

"Help people manage the content and organisation of their desktop: Most people are hopeless at personal content management but don't want to admit it. Provide them with a desktop search tool and show them how to use it effectively.

Help people identify and use the most appropriate communication tool: Give them a one-page cheat sheet on when not to use e-mail and why not, and what to use instead. Create a simple 'tool-chooser' or decision tree with links to where they can learn more about each tool available.

Teach people how to do research, not just search: If people are going to do their own research, they need to learn how to do it competently. Most of the people I know can't."

Then they need the opportunity

The most powerful tools in the world won't help if you don't have the time or the authority to use them. The second ingredient of an effective bottom-up learning strategy is **opportunity**:

Discretionary time: Bottom-up learning is in most cases a discretionary activity for which time must be made available. Many employees – particularly knowledge workers – have some degree of discretion about how they spend their time; others are strictly

---

[40] *Knowledge management: Finding quick wins and long term value* by Dave Pollard, a posting to his *How to Save the World* blog, March 29, 2007 – http://blogs.salon.com/0002007/2007/03/29.html

rostered and timetabled and can only participate in bottom-up learning activities outside work hours or in time specially allocated by their managers.

Authority: Time is not the only issue – even with the time, employees have to be allowed to contribute to bottom-up learning, whether that's through formal organisational policies or the specific inclusion of these activities in their job descriptions. L&d professionals have their role to play here, by making sure that their own policies don't leave all the power to control the teaching and learning process in their own hands. A good example would be the restrictions that are often placed on the content that can be published on an organisation's LMS, making it impossible for rapid or user-generated content to be distributed in this way.

Informal spaces provide those without the facility or the inclination to blog with a face-to-face equivalent. Americans talk about the learning that takes place 'around the water cooler' and with good reason. Coffee areas and staff restaurants have the same effect, as do the areas where smokers gather to satisfy their addictions. Organisations create these spaces primarily for their functional purpose, but they should also be aware of the learning opportunities that these provide.

Experts in the open: throughout history, humans have learned a great deal by observing experts in their everyday work. Organisations can facilitate this process by arranging workspaces in such a way that novices can work alongside the experts, much as apprentices and their masters have done for centuries.

And then they need the motive

As any reader of detective novels will know, any self-respecting criminal needs the means, the motive and the opportunity. Now no-one's suggesting that employees should behave like criminals, but they should be given every chance to learn. We're left with the issue of **motive**:

Intrinsic motivation: Bottom-up learning is most likely to occur if an employee has a desire to improve their performance, or at least to maintain their performance in the face of changing circumstances. Without motivation, the motive has to be externally provided.

Modelling: One of the most powerful influences on our behaviour is the example provided by others that we respect. If managers and high profile peers exhibit the behaviour of effective bottom-up teachers and learners, then the pattern is established.

Tangible rewards: Ideally, those employees that contribute most to their own development and to the learning of those around them will benefit from this is some tangible way, whether that's through an increase in pay or through a promotion. To make the connection between learning and reward absolutely clear, it makes sense for this to be explicitly included in an organisation's performance management policy.

Intangible rewards: A reward does not have to be bankable to act as a powerful incentive; often all that's needed is a little recognition, whether that's from managers or peers. An employee whose manager thanks them for taking the initiative in meeting their own learning needs or by helping to meet those of their peers, will be only too keen to repeat the process.

Remember that it is natural for human beings to co-operate with each other, whether on a 'I'll scratch your back if you scratch mine' basis, or because a goal can only be achieved though combined effort. We are usually quite happy to share expertise, to be a teacher as well as a learner – it's flattering to us. Too much in the way of external incentive may only cause suspicion; too little and it looks like this behaviour is not valued by the organisation.

Conditions for success

To summarise, these are the conditions for success with bottom-up learning:

- Bottom-up learning is not relied upon to meet needs that are critical or common to large numbers of employees.
- The appropriate tools are put in place to support bottom-up learning.
- Where necessary, employees are provided with the right training to help them to use these tools.
- Employees have sufficient discretionary time to devote to bottom-up learning.
- Employees are provided with the authority to engage in bottom-up learning activities.
- Workspaces are designed to encourage informal communication and to maximise the opportunities for novices to observe experts at work.
- Managers and respected peers model effective bottom-up learning behaviour.
- The performance management policy encourages bottom-up learning.

- Employees are recognised for taking the initiative in meeting their own learning needs and in helping peers to meet their needs.

When the culture is not supportive right at the top, then chances are diminished but not destroyed. Cultures can differ in divisions or departments, under strong leadership. A learning and development department may influence the culture, through the programmes that it offers (including leadership development programmes and executive coaching), but does not have the mandate to unilaterally change a culture. This must come from the organisation's leadership.

Profile: Peter Butler

This profile shows how, with the right vision and leadership, a large multinational company can successfully establish a bottom-up learning culture, in this case with the aid of the latest social learning technologies. Peter's work with Dare2Share has demonstrated what can be achieved within what many would regard as a relatively traditional management hierarchy.

Peter Butler was for six years Learning Director at British Telecom, a major international telecommunications company with 160,000 employees and contractors, about 1/3 of which are based outside the UK. When he started the job, Peter set up a governance process embodied in the BT Learning Council which he chaired and which oversaw some £70m annually in direct training costs. Peter talked to each of the BT businesses and developed learning plans aligned with the strategic direction of each business. Initial priorities of the Learning Council were to rationalise down from 14 learning management systems to one, establish an evaluation strategy, develop an online learning planning tool, and to create a single system for procurement.

Phase two was to move from what Peter called "getting things fixed" to "doing things more effectively." At the heart of this was Peter's commitment to "breaking through the walls of the classroom" and embedding learning on the job. To encourage new ideas, he ran an innovation day in which a number of new proposals were put forward. One was selected for piloting – the use of social learning.

The place for formal learning

In starting to look at new, more informal techniques, Peter was not trying to replace formal training. Rather, he wanted the decision to engage in formal training to be more rational and explicit. He acknowledges that health and safety, regulatory and compliance training are business critical for BT, also that sometimes it is highly beneficial to bring people together off-the-job as with leadership development.

When it comes to induction and apprenticeship, Peter believes the mix has to extend beyond the formal. He would be more inclined to provide 'learning nuggets' in advance of their first day of work and to support formal courses with mentoring.

Daring to share

Peter is an advocate for hiring motivated young people and then coaching them to come through the ranks with the emphasis on informal learning in the workplace. He finds the emphasis on formal knowledge management techniques funny: "If you have the word 'management' in the title then that implies control and interference, and as a result people will be less likely to use it."

BT's *Dare2Share* platform takes the opposite, bottom-up approach. "Dare2Share means we are proud to let employees know how clever they are – the less management the better. After all, no-one determined what went up on YouTube. The idea is to create the right system and then let people use it as they see best. Just like YouTube we use peer ratings to help users determine what's good to watch."

Peter believes that what drives people to create video content – and video features heavily on *Dare2Share* – is the excitement around a newly-accessible medium. "The biggest incentive is seeing their mate on the screen, then wanting to do it themselves. That's how young people think. And it's important for l&d managers to keep their minds young. Ask yourself, when was the last time you watched your children learning? When did you last ask them why they use new technologies? You can't understand social learning without participating in it."

The project started with a proof of concept with just a few contributors, then moved on to a more widespread pilot over 6-8 weeks. There was some concern about the impact of so much video content on the network, which was justified when the system had 13,000 users within a few weeks. As a result the system had to be upgraded before launch to the population as a whole.

In practice, *Dare2Share* has become much more than Peter expected, hosting top-down learning nuggets, such as the *50 Lessons* business series and messages from senior leaders, as well as content produced by employees. Although perhaps only 3-5% of employees do contribute content, this is in line with accepted averages and Peter is quite happy with this. With such a large workforce, this means a steady supply of new material from which the whole organisation can benefit.

Solving real business problems

BT has some of the finest research and development facilities available anywhere, so Peter is well aware of the fantastic advances in technology that we can expect in the near future. On the other hand he is mindful of the danger of latching onto a solution and then looking for a problem. As a result his priority is to work back from an identified business problem to look for creative solutions. He can see how BT's thousands of engineers in the field could connect with one another to solve problems at the point of need and then capture that expertise for use in the future. He also knows that many of the problems which cause customers to call in for help could be resolved easily if learning content was made more available to them. He is conscious that the emphasis is shifting from pushing information at people to providing resources from which they can pull as the need arises. This will require search capabilities as extensive and powerful as Google's, accessing material not only within the confines of a learning management system but across all available sources, including platforms like *Dare2Share*. This is a future that BT is well established to realise.

Peter Butler joined Lloyds Banking Group in October 2010 as learning director. Before his appointment he served as Director of Learning, BT Group plc from June 2004. He joined BT from RBS and was a formerly at NatWest prior to the merger in 2000. He was retained after the merger to bring together the learning teams in the respective banks. His previous experience included executive development, senior HR roles in the Retail business, corporate and commercial banking and a variety of HR roles.

His role in BT included chair of the Learning Council, the governing body responsible for the £70m annual spend, the acclaimed apprenticeship programme, where he secured £17m of government funding, and responsibility for the learning technology strategy and in particular the "social learning" agenda.

He is on the advisory board for the Skills Minister and was a key player in support of the IT & Telecoms sector skills council's bid for funding to create the National Skills Academy for IT.

Formal learning

Having explored the contextual model from top to bottom, it is time to begin a closer examination of the four main contexts in which learning takes place in the workplace, starting with formal learning. Why start with the fourth of the contexts, rather than working from left to right? Well, simply because formal learning is what most people focus on when they think about learning at work. For many, learning means courses, and typically it means those courses where teachers and trainers provide instruction to a group of learners in a classroom.

The characteristics of formal learning

Both formal and non-formal learning are proactive approaches, with the same overall goal of equipping employees with the knowledge and skills that they require to meet present and future job responsibilities. The difference with formal learning is in the way that this task is tackled.

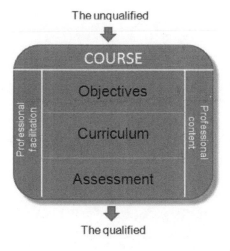

Formal learning experiences are typically packaged as 'courses' or 'programmes'. These tend to have a number of features in common:

- **Objectives** that describe, in terms of knowledge, skills and attitudinal change, what learning is intended to result from successful completion of the course or programme. Some courses may adopt a more learner-centred approach, focusing on the goals of the learners themselves, but it would still be highly unlikely for a formal learning intervention to have no objectives at all, whether or not these are made explicit.
- An established **curriculum** or learning plan, which sets out how the learning objectives are to be achieved in terms of the topics to be covered and/or the activities to be undertaken.
- **Content** assembled by or with reference to acknowledged subject experts. At the very least this content is likely to consist of a simple trainer guide or lecture notes. More commonly, it will extend to slides, videos and other visual aids, handouts, job aids and reference books. And where self-study forms an important part of the intervention, the content could include workbooks, online reference materials, interactive tutorials and simulations.
- A designated **teacher, trainer or tutor** to facilitate the learning process. The role of this person or persons will vary widely depending on the type of intervention and pedagogical approach, from a formal instructor to a subject expert, a coach, an assessor, a moderator or a curator. In cases where the intervention consists entirely of unsupported self-study, there will, of course, be no role at all.

- Some form of **assessment**, to determine whether the learning objectives have been achieved. Where a qualification is being awarded, this assessment could be elaborate, requiring an exam, a practical assessment, or the formal submission of a paper or portfolio. In other cases, the process of assessment could be much less formal, perhaps a practical exercise or a quiz.

When formal learning does the job

The structure inherent in formal education, training and development provides advantages for employers and employees alike:

- Because the curriculum is formally laid out in advance, employers can have greater confidence that important content has been covered consistently.

- Because a formalised intervention has a clear beginning and end, employers can more easily track who has had what training and when.

- Because of the assessment process, employers can have greater confidence that learning objectives have actually been achieved.

- Because professional facilitators are leading the intervention, employees can have greater confidence in the quality of the tuition they are likely to receive.

- Because content is sourced from subject experts and assembled by professionals, employees are more likely to have access to high quality materials.

- Because the intervention has a recognised outcome, even if that is just a formal completion, employees have the opportunity to gain a certification/qualification that may be valuable in their careers.

Of course, few of these advantages can be guaranteed; a great deal depends on the skill with which the intervention is targeted, designed and delivered. However, it is easy to see why employers and employees are likely to have more confidence in a formalised intervention than any less formal alternative, particularly when the stakes are high:

- When an employer needs to be able to demonstrate compliance to an external regulator.

- When a high degree of proficiency is absolutely vital to avoid the chance of an expensive error, damage to an employer's reputation, or risk to health and safety. Quite clearly we cannot rely on informal learning processes to provide the skills needed by airline pilots, surgeons or structural engineers. These may be exceptional cases, but there are elements in most jobs where proficiency cannot be left to chance.

- When an employee is a complete novice and depends on a structured approach to their initial training.

- When the attainment of a qualification can make a big difference to an employee's career progression.

However strong the lobby for more informal approaches to workplace learning, it is hard to see how we could do without formal learning altogether. The problem is not with the concept of formal learning; it is with the assumption, often held by l&d professionals, their internal 'clients' and learners themselves, that every learning and development requirement is best addressed by a course. As they say, when you've got a hammer in your hand, every problem looks like a nail.

When formal learning is less appropriate

What is the difference between education and training? The answer, according to the old joke, is that, whereas you might be happy for your children to have sex education at school, you'd be a little disconcerted if they had sex training. Training is, almost by definition, interactive. It has to impact on performance and, to accomplish this, it must involve a highly practical element.

In a formal learning situation, teachers, coaches, instructional designers and other 'learning experts' take on the responsibility not only for providing interesting new learning material but also for assisting the learner to recognise what's important, transfer this to long-term memory and then strengthen their pathways to this new learning. They achieve this primarily through interaction – questions, exercises, discussions, essays, assignments, and so on.

But it's a mistake to believe that learning can only take place when this interaction is externally mediated; individuals can also do this for themselves. Those who have learned how to learn are capable of acting independently: they can recognise when something is important, they reflect, they make notes, initiate conversations and post to their blogs. They're also quite capable on acting on what they have learned by applying it to their jobs. With independent learners, courses with formalised interactions will often not be necessary.

In 1992, Hubert Dreyfus[41] described the journey that learners take from 'novice' to 'advanced beginner' to 'competent' to 'proficient'

---

[41] *Mind Over Machine* by Herbert Dreyfus, 1992.

to 'expert'. Brian Sutton[42] explains how different approaches are required at different stages along this journey: "The transition from novice to advanced beginner is essentially associated with rule following behaviour and this is best facilitated through formal learning processes. However, the transition from competent through proficient to expert is largely associated with pattern recognition and experience. It can only be attained within the performance context. It is rooted in the acquisition and sharing of tacit knowledge and this is fundamentally a social process – it needs prolonged and deep engagement with other expert practitioners."

Sutton goes further to argue that "...as learning professionals we need to stop thinking of learning as an event that is organised by one set of people and imposed upon another, regardless of whether that event takes place in a classroom or via the medium of e-learning. Learning is a natural consequence of living and working: work has always involved problem solving, judgement, conflict resolution and choice – these are all learning opportunities. We can experience them and move on regardless or we can reflect upon them within the context of our environment and our core principles and, as a result, produce new insights that move us forward."

There is a price to pay for the structure inherent in formal learning: interventions take time, money and expertise to design and develop. Organisations can't always afford to wait for the interventions to be made available, nor can they necessarily spare the resources. When the learning is important to the organisation, when there is a sufficiently large target audience, when there is adequate lead time, then the investment might be made. When

---

[42] *Learning's Environmental Crisis* by Brian Sutton, published as part of the Advance series by Saffron Interactive, 2007.

these conditions aren't met, the organisation can either look for an off-the-shelf solution from an external supplier or adopt a more informal approach.

The inflexibility of formal learning can extend to the content, as John Seely Brown and Paul Duquid observe[43]: "Learning is usually treated as a supply-side matter, thought to follow teaching, training or information delivery. But learning is much more demand driven. People learn in response to need. When people cannot see the need for what's being taught, they ignore it, reject it, or fail to assimilate it in any meaningful way. Conversely, when they have a need, then, if the resources for learning are available, people learn effectively and quickly."

Sometimes, as Harold Jarche[44] likes to say, you need the ABC solution; that's Anything But Courses.

The transfer of learning

A formal learning intervention is only successful if it results in lasting change in the learner's behaviour on the job. In their 1992 book *Transfer of Training*, Mary Broad and John Newstrom[45] estimated that "...merely 10% of the training dollars spent result in actual and lasting behavioural change."

When assessing what made the biggest impact on transfer of learning, the authors looked at three different parties – the learner's manager, the trainer/facilitator and the learner themselves – at three stages in the process – before the

---

[43] *The Social Life of Information* by John Seely Brown and Paul Duquid, Harvard Business School Press, 2002.
[44] *Learning & Working on the Web*, December 30, 2008:
http://www.jarche.com/2008/12/innovation-and-learning/.
[45] *Transfer of Training* by Mary Broad and John Newstrom, Basic Books, 1992

intervention, during and after. They found that the greatest impact was made by the learner's manager in setting expectations before the intervention; next most important was the trainer's role before the intervention in getting to know the needs of the learners they would be training; third most important was the manager's role after the intervention.

	Before	During	After
Learner's manager	1	8	3
The trainer / facilitator	2	4	9
The learner themselves	7	5	6

Strategies for formal learning

Formal learning comes in many shapes and sizes. The effectiveness and efficiency with which a formal learning intervention is delivered depends to a large extent on whether the shape and the size are appropriate for the job.

Clark and Wittrock[46] devised a useful model for analysing training strategies according to the degree of control imposed over the learning process by the trainer and/or the student. At the most trainer-centred end of the spectrum is simple **exposition** – the trainer tells the learner things, using methods such as lectures or prescribed reading; no interaction is expected or required, except perhaps some Q&A or an assessment.

---

[46] *Psychological Principles of Training* by Ruth Clark and Merlin C Wittrock, published in *Training and Retraining*, Macmillan Reference USA (2001).

The second strategy – **structured instruction** – is still under the trainer's overall control, but is much more interactive, allowing the trainer to fine-tune the process to the needs of the particular audience. Structured instruction is widely used in training, and includes most classroom sessions and most computer-based self-study materials. Novices will rely on this degree of structure; independent learners can often do without.

A more learner-centred strategy is **guided discovery**. In this case, learners engage in tasks that have been specially designed to provide them with opportunities to experiment with alternative approaches. Learners improve their skill or understanding by reflecting, with the help of facilitators, coaches or mentors, upon the outcomes of these tasks and, as a result, drawing general conclusions which they can apply to future tasks. Guided discovery allows learners to have a go and learn from their mistakes. This strategy can be deployed in the classroom, in outdoor settings (as with Outward Bound-style courses) or through computer-based case studies, games and simulations.

The final strategy in Clark and Wittrock's model is **exploration**. Here each learner determines their own learning process, taking advantage of resources provided by trainers and others, and takes out of this process their own, unique learning. Exploration may seem a relatively informal strategy, but can be integrated into formalised interventions as a component in a blended solution.

A formal learning intervention may rely on just one of these strategies, but increasingly will use a combination. The choice of strategy will depend on the nature of the learning objectives, the prior knowledge and the expectations of the target audience and, to some extent, the preferences and values of the trainer.

Social contexts for formal learning

Learning can take place in a variety of social contexts ranging from self-study through to learning in large groups. These contexts have a major impact on the effectiveness of the intervention and so some care must be taken in choosing the right social context, or combination of contexts, for each intervention.

The learner alone: When the learner works alone they enjoy an obvious increase in flexibility – they can determine when they learn and for how long, the pace of the learning, and the location. We know from surveys that learners value the ability to control the pace of their learning above all other factors. We also know that they value being able to learn in small, digestible chunks.

On the other hand, self-study has its drawbacks. Unless specific deadlines are set, the learner has to make all the running in terms of motivation, a difficult task when you consider that learning is rarely that urgent, and must compete with a myriad of short-term priorities. There's also the problem of isolation: unless the self-study activity is supported, the learner has no-one with whom they can discuss issues or resolve any misunderstandings. And without a group of peers, learners have no access to alternative perspectives and experiences, and don't receive the additional motivational boost that comes with peer pressure.

Self-study is being used more and more for formal learning, typically through the medium of interactive online materials. This approach can work well for shorter courses, but has limitations when the learning is more complex and multi-faceted, and when engagement with trainers and peers is critical to the outcome. In these cases self-study may still play a role, but only as an element within a blend.

Learning one-to-one: When used for the right purpose and well executed, one-to-one learning can be more effective than any other approach; that's because the learner has the undivided attention of a full-time instructor/coach/mentor, who can adapt their responses to the particular needs of the individual learner.

There are limitations to the approach however: the low trainer-to-learner ratio is time-consuming and therefore slow and highly expensive; and there are also obvious limitations on the activities that can be carried out, given the absence of a group of learners.

One-to-one learning is unlikely to be used as the principal approach in a formal learning intervention, although it is widely used in more informal situations such as on-job training and coaching. Its primary use in formal learning is as an ingredient in a blended solution.

Learning in groups: Most of the formal learning that we have encountered has been in groups, typically in a classroom. By learning in groups we experience some powerful advantages: we can share experiences and perspectives, we can engage in discussions, we can work together on practical activities, we can share each other's successes and disappointments.

Where group events fall down is when they are used as a way to deliver large quantities of information. Unless a group is wholly homogeneous, which is practically an impossibility, some learners will be lagging behind and some will be frustrated at the slow pace; some will be interested in the topic and some not; some will want to ask lots of questions, others will not have the confidence. And when these events are face-to-face, the likelihood is that they will go on for far too long and cause cognitive overload for just about every participant.

Undoubtedly group learning will continue to play a dominant role in formal learning, even if more of this switches to online delivery and an element becomes asynchronous (using tools such as email, blogs and forums).

Each of the three social contexts provides us with considerable scope to employ a wide range of educational and training methods, as shown by the table below:

The learner alone	Learning one-to-one	Learning in groups
Reading	Receiving instruction	Receiving lectures / presentations
Planning		
Reflecting	Receiving subject-matter support	Receiving instruction
Researching		Receiving subject-matter support
Completing questionnaires	Receiving coaching	
	Receiving mentoring	Engaging in discussions
Completing interactive lessons	Reviewing progress	Engaging in group problem-solving activities
Problem-solving		
Viewing recorded video		Engaging in multi-player games and simulations
Listening to recorded audio		
Participating in single-player games and simulations		Engaging in role plays and other practical exercises
Completing drill and practice exercises		Visiting other departments / organisations

Completing assessments	Undertaking group assignments / projects
Undertaking assignments / projects	Engaging in group progress reviews
Visiting other departments / organisations	Networking
Work experience	Collaborating on content development (e g with a wiki)
Using performance support / reference materials	

Interestingly, the methods listed above are practically timeless – the list would have been much the same a hundred years ago, perhaps a thousand. Only a few of the methods are dependent on any technology: reading, obviously, which required the invention of printing; and viewing video and listening to audio would not have been possible until some form of recording mechanism was developed. Although the range of methods doesn't change much, the choices we make amongst them most certainly do, influenced by advances in educational psychology and neuroscience, political viewpoints, fashions and the changing expectations of next generation learners.

But these choices really do matter. As Sitzmann et al[47] confirmed, ultimately it's the instructional method, not the delivery medium that makes the difference. When web-based instruction and

---

[47] *The comparative effectiveness of web-based and classroom instruction: a meta-analysis* by T Sitzmann, K Kraiger, D Stewart and R Wisher, published in Personnel Psychology (2006).

classroom instruction that have similar methods were compared, there was little or no difference in outcomes. Thomas L. Russell[48] undertook an analysis of more than 350 studies conducted over the past 50 years, each attempting to compare the effectiveness of one learning medium with another. The title of Russell's book is The No Significant Difference Phenomenon, which says it all.

Media for formal learning

In contrast to educational and training methods, the options in terms of learning media are growing exponentially. If methods have the main impact on the effectiveness of a learning intervention, then media have the main influence on efficiency – the way in which resources are used to deliver the learning outcomes. The possibilities for efficiencies have grown enormously with advances in technology.

Not all learning is mediated – as we have seen, much is incidental and reflective – but in the context of a formal intervention, media selections will always have to be made. The options have increased over time. All learning was, of course, originally conducted face-to-face, providing an immediacy to the interaction, a rich sensory experience (you see, you hear, you touch, you smell) and, if you're lucky enough to be one-on-one, the ultimate in personalisation.

Books, when they arrived, provided the counterbalance, by allowing learners more independence and the ability to control the pace. The invention of the telephone provided additional connectivity for learners and tutors working at a distance. Videos, CDs and all their variants added to the diversity of offline media

---

[48] *The No Significant Difference Phenomenon* by Thomas L. Russell, online at http://www.nosignificantdifference.org/.

and made high-quality audio and video available to distance learners.

But perhaps the most significant new medium made available by technology is the networked computer, connecting learners to more than a billion other internet users and countless billions of web pages. 'E-learning' is the rather inadequate name we give to the use of computer networks as a channel to facilitate learning. This channel supports a wide range of synchronous and asynchronous media, as shown below:

Synchronous (real-time) online media	Asynchronous (self-paced) online media
Chat rooms	Email
Instant messaging	Web pages
Web conferencing	Downloadable documents and media files
Multi-player virtual worlds	Forums
	Blogs
	Wikis
	Social networks
	Single-player virtual worlds

Top-down approaches

Formal learning is most commonly organised on a top-down basis by employers for their employees. They have a wide range of options at their disposal:

Classroom courses

Medium: face-to-face/synchronous.
Social context: group.
Typical strategies: exposition (particularly in higher education), structured instruction and guided discovery.

Until about 10 years ago, the overwhelming majority of formal learning took place in classrooms. Since then, other approaches, particularly those that employ technology, have significantly eaten in to this share, but it is probable that still more than 50% of courses are classroom based.

Classrooms are versatile environments in which to provide training, supporting a wide range of strategies and training methods: the trainer is able to augment their own delivery with flip charts, whiteboards, slides, videos, models and printed materials; participants can be divided into small groups to undertake practical exercises; and classrooms can be equipped with PCs so each participant can work individually to develop their IT skills, while under the supervision of the trainer. And because they are off-job, classrooms are free from normal day-to-day interruptions and provide a rare opportunity for protected learning time.

The danger in a classroom is that the trainer dominates proceedings in their role as 'performance artist.' As Professor

Dylan Wiliam[49] explains: "Teachers do not create learning. Learners create learning. Teachers create the conditions under which learning can take place. Our schools don't function like that, which is why somebody once joked that schools are places where kids go to watch teachers work."

The transition from 'sage on the stage' to 'guide on the side' is recognised by l&d professionals themselves, as indicated in a CIPD report[50]: "Trainers are no longer the sun around which learning planets revolve. Training should no longer be seen as a discrete set of activities around a course or similar event."

Classroom courses are:

- *at their best when* collaborative, practical, learner-centred and facilitated by skilled trainers;
- *best avoided when* they last for more than a few days at a time, are focused primarily on knowledge transfer, are trainer-centred.

Outdoor learning

Medium: face-to-face/synchronous.
Social context: group.
Typical strategies: guided discovery.

Outdoor learning extends the classroom into the great outdoors, where a wider range of activities can be undertaken, typically for team-building and leadership development. Most outdoor learning is experiential: participants are allocated to groups and are set

---

[49] From a presentation given by Prof. Dylan Wiliam to the Association for Learning technology, 2007.
[50] *Supporting, accelerating and directing learning* from the Chartered Institute of Personnel and Development, 2008.

tasks, perhaps crossing a lake or building a shelter; when the task has been completed they then review how they went about the task and make new generalisations about the process they should follow in future.

Outdoor learning is:

- *at its best when* voluntary, open in terms of outcomes, designed to suit all ages and fitness levels, facilitated by skilled trainers;
- *best avoided when* mandatory, contrived in terms of outcomes, overly demanding physically.

Self-study e-learning

Medium: online/asynchronous.
Social context: individual.
Typical strategies: normally structured instruction, sometimes simple exposition.

Self-study e-learning might sound like a recent invention, but in fact has its origins in the computer-assisted learning of the late 1970s. Although delivery has shifted from floppy disks to laserdiscs to CD-ROMs to web browsers, the essential model is the same: the learner works alone, progressing at their own pace through a series of lessons delivered by the computer. These lessons are likely to include expositions of learning content – using text, graphics, and sometimes animation, audio or video – as well as questions, exercises and assessments.

When well-designed, self-study e-learning can be engaging and highly-effective; it delivers content clearly and consistently; it can provide multiple opportunities for practice and provide instant and individualised feedback. Although relatively time-consuming and expensive to develop, self-study materials require little support during delivery and can therefore be highly cost-effective for larger audiences. And evidence of progress and achievement can be automatically recorded using a learning management system.

At its worst, self-study e-learning can be tedious, text-heavy and lacking in meaningful interaction. Clearly this is not a problem inherent in the medium, but rather a consequence of poor design skills. Having said that, these design skills are not easy to acquire and the majority of l&d professionals would probably rather leave this work to enthusiasts and specialists.

Self-study e-learning is:

- *at its best when* clear and to the point, relevant to the job, highly interactive and well supported by relevant images and multimedia;
- *best avoided when* the subject is unsuited to self-study, when it's long and laborious, when text-heavy and short on meaningful, challenging interactivity.

Collaborative distance learning

Medium: online/synchronous and asynchronous.
Social context: individual, one-to-one and group.
Typical strategies: exposition, guided discovery, exploration.

The use of the internet as a tool for distance learning has evolved primarily in further and higher education, particularly in support of part-time students working towards postgraduate degrees and professional certifications. A typical collaborative distance learning course is likely to include the following:

- Learning materials (web pages, downloadable documents, links, videos, podcasts, etc.) hosted on a virtual learning environment such as Moodle, Blackboard or Desire2Learn.

- A forum which students can use to communicate with each other asynchronously, to discuss issues, collaborate on group tasks and share their work. More recently, virtual learning environments have been extended to allow facilities for student blogging and collaboration using wikis.

- Some form of synchronous communication tool, at the very least a text chat facility, but more likely now to be web conferencing, to allow real-time discussion and the delivery of presentations.

- A facility to upload assignments for grading by a tutor.

If it is well-designed and facilitated, online distance learning can provide students with a rich and rewarding learning experience, combining individual and group work with the facility for one-to-one support from a tutor, and supporting a wide range of learning strategies. Many courses achieve wonderful results, but in the worst cases students are presented with little more than online lecture notes for materials, poor support and little in the way of meaningful collaboration.

Collaborative distance learning is:

- *at its best when* it mixes self-paced and live activities, it encourages group collaboration, it runs to a strict schedule, is well facilitated;

- *best avoided when* it consists mainly of self-study, the materials are dull, there is little contact with the facilitator.

Electronic games and simulations

Medium: desktop or online applications/synchronous or asynchronous.
Social context: individual or group.
Typical strategies: guided discovery, exploration.

Games and simulations can run on a wide variety of platforms, from PCs to handheld devices to video games consoles. They can be aimed at individual use (in which case they are asynchronous) or for use by groups (typically synchronous). When intended for single players, they can run directly from the local computer; when they are multi-player, they need to have an online capability.

Games and simulations are, of course, not the same thing. A game is an activity with a goal and with rules, in which the learner competes against others, real or imaginary, or to better their own, previous attainments. A simulation, on the other hand is, according to the Wikipedia, 'an imitation of some real thing, state of affairs, or process'. It enables learners to experiment, make mistakes, experience successes, obtain feedback, reflect and hypothesise. To be effective, simulations need to approximate the situation in which the skill must be applied for real. This requires a degree of *physical fidelity* (the simulation looks and feels like the real thing) and *functional fidelity* (it behaves like the real thing). Fidelity comes at a cost (many millions of dollars if you're talking flight simulators or similar, many hundreds of thousands if you're looking to enact a critical incident with multiple players in a virtual world) but cost has, of course, to be balanced against risk. The degree of physical or functional fidelity that you need will also depend on the type of skill that you're looking to address – cognitive, motor, interpersonal, or some combination of these.

Games can involve simulation, as with classic business games and strategy games of the Sim-City variety, but they can take many other forms as well, centring on quizzes, adventures or puzzles. Simulations can include elements of game play, such as goals, rules, levels or competition, but can happily exist without any of these, as environments for experimentation, reflection, practice and discovery.

Single player games and simulations provide many of the practical advantages of self-study e-learning, but can provide a much more engaging and immersive experience. Multi-player games and simulations have more of the character of classroom or outdoor learning.

A growing trend is to use 3D computer graphics to generate a virtual world as a setting for the game or simulation. On games consoles, 3D has been the norm for something like 15 years, but development costs have been out of reach for all but the most critical training applications and the use of 3D graphics has placed heavy demands on the performance of the learner's computer. More recently, we have begun to see a range of new authoring tools coming on to the market which reduce the barriers to entry substantially. At the same time, most modern PCs are now able to meet the demands of 3D graphics with ease.

It is unlikely that a game or simulation would constitute the entirety of a formal learning intervention, although it may well be the central element. More typically, a game or simulation will be supported by introductory materials, debriefings and instructional materials that will fill in any gaps evidenced during game play.

Electronic games and simulations are:

- *at their best when* they behave like the real world does, look like the real world too, allow for repeated practice, help learners to learn from their mistakes;
- *best avoided when* used as another way of conveying knowledge, behave unconvincingly, are poorly supported.

Blended solutions

Medium: a variety of synchronous and asynchronous media.
Social context: a variety of contexts.
Typical strategies: a variety of strategies.

There is no widespread agreement on a definition for blended learning. Are we talking about a blend of strategies, a blend of methods or a blend of media? Does e-learning have to be one of the elements in the blend? Are we actually talking about blended teaching rather than blended learning? Given that the latter is more often the case, I put forward my own rather wordy summary[51]:

"A blended learning solution combines educational and training methods within different social contexts for learning (self-study, one-to-one, group), with the aim of increasing learning effectiveness. It may also mix the learning media used to deliver the solution (face-to-face, online, offline, telephonic, etc.) as a way to optimise the efficiency of the solution. These choices are made in response to particular learning requirements, audience characteristics, and practical constraints and opportunities."

---

[51] *The Blended Learning Cookbook*, second edition, by Clive Shepherd, Saffron Interactive, 2008.

Given this definition, it is clear that there is nothing new in the concept of blended learning, although it would be fair to say that, until recently, only a small proportion of interventions were actually blended. It may well be that the need for blending has only really become evident now that viable alternatives to the classroom have become available. Many employers may have switched emphasis to self-study approaches, probably online, only to discover that they had probably thrown the baby out with the bathwater. The reality is that all major social contexts for learning and all principle media options have as many disadvantages as they have advantages. Often the only way that the advantages can be exploited and the disadvantages avoided is by employing a combination of approaches, making sure that the right tool is used for each task.

Because, by definition, blended solutions contain a number of elements, they are more difficult to implement than solutions which are based on a single approach. For that reason, blending is not going to be appropriate for simple applications of limited duration. Where a blend makes most sense is when the learning requirement is multi-faceted, the audience is heterogeneous and there are numerous practical constraints to be overcome.

Above all, blended solutions provide the opportunity to create interventions that deliver a complete learning experience, grounded in real-world problems and resulting in real-world application. Too many formal learning interventions do a good job of engaging the learner for a limited period and creating an interest in a topic or skill; where they fall down is in the process that follows, when skills have to honed and refined, and learning tested against the realities of the real world. A well-designed blend will draw on approaches more usually associated with other contexts –

non-formal, on-demand and experiential – to bridge the gap from theory to practice.

Blended solutions are:

- *at their best when* they maintain a good balance between live and self-paced activities, when they create a bridge between formalised and informal learning;
- *best avoided when* used purely as a cost-cutting exercise, are overly complex.

Bottom-up approaches

It might seem odd to conceive of formal learning interventions as being anything other than top-down, but there are frequent occasions when the initiative to undertake a course comes from the employee and not the employer. Principally this will occur when the employee wishes to obtain some form of technical or professional accreditation that will enhance their career prospects. Most employers operate some form of scheme to at least part fund these courses, sometimes with provisions for return of this subsidy if the employee subsequently leaves their job before a certain date.

Otherwise, formal learning that is initiated from a bottom-up perspective can take any of the forms described above under top-down.

Conditions for success

To enjoy success with formal learning it is necessary for the l&d professional to recognise the following:

- that not all learning needs to be packaged up as a course – more informal approaches are often perfectly adequate;

- that there are many means available for the delivery of courses, not just classroom delivery;
- that sometimes no single approach will do the job and that a blended solution will be necessary;
- that learning must be a process embedded in workplace performance, not an event;
- that trainers are more likely to be effective as 'guides on the side' than as 'sages on the stage'.

Profile: Julie Wedgwood

In our next profile we meet Julie Wedgwood who, almost single-handedly, transformed a very traditional IT training team into enthusiastic innovators capable of showing that formal training can be flexible, effective and fun.

In January 2008, Julie Wedgwood commenced working with the Cheshire ICT Service, which provides support for 10,500 National Health Service employees across the county of Cheshire in the UK. This shared service had been formed by bringing together the IT departments from three major NHS trusts. At the time, the HR function for the three trusts was also re-constituted as a shared service, although there was no real engagement by the l&d department with Julie's ICT team. As Julie recalls, at one of her first encounters with HR, when she hinted at the changes she would like to see made, she was asked, "What on earth is someone like you doing in the NHS?" This was going to be tough.

Change begins with the team

In re-inventing the formal course curriculum, Julie was inspired by the words of Professor Stephen Heppel, who famously advised teachers not to "Do a Dick Turpin." For those of you unfamiliar with this character from UK folklore, Dick was a highwayman who commanded those unfortunate travellers that he waylaid to "stand and deliver". Julie felt that the lecture approach to delivering learning within the NHS was no longer practical or effective.

On the other hand, as Julie explained, "Our experience of being taught is how we expect to teach." Most of the trainers had built their career by following this approach and it was, to some degree, expected by Julie that they would be resistant to the changes she was proposing as well as a little fearful that the NHS staff would not accept or warm to a more blended strategy of delivery. Julie wanted to help the trainers realise that 'a tick in the box was no longer enough' and that, by changing, they could make their training much more effective and meaningful. Julie suggested they held up a mirror and asked themselves whether people really were walking away from their training with changed behaviour.

This change was accomplished without the support of management who, according to Julie, "didn't know what they were asking for and just wanted training to work as a service. They didn't realise that training could have a positive impact on their business or that effective training could make people feel good about their organisation."

Julie created a three-year blended learning strategy which, although approved by the Board, suffered budget cuts of 75%: "Management didn't emotionally connect with it, they just said do it." It became apparent that change had to occur by stealth, from the bottom-up, and that meant starting with the training team.

For Julie, their commitment was vital: "All trainers do is communicate. If they are not communicating positively about the changes they are being asked to make then they will sabotage them." She invited the whole team to accompany her to the Learning Technologies exhibition in London. Many made their excuses on the day and, of the two who did come, one dropped the bombshell at the end of the day: "Thank you for a nice day out in London but I'm resigning tomorrow." Undeterred, Julie created a programme of development for the trainers ('21 Lessons') which introduced a wide range of learning technologies to them, challenging and encouraging them to engage with and use them as part of their new blended learning delivery. A key element of the programme was to get the training team to collaborate with each other and this proved to be enormously influential in changing both the trainers and the organisation's view of what training should and could be like.

Julie also made a point of going out and engaging with key stakeholders across the business, listening to what it was they really needed. She wanted to be able to understand their language, their priorities and the practicalities they faced. She profiled each audience and shaped the operational plan accordingly, realising that she needed a delivery mechanism that the middle management would commit to.

The new offering

Julie decided against a big bang approach, bringing change in slowly and helping both learners and trainers to ease into a new way of learning. The NHS was still very course focused, so Julie decided not to fight this head-on initially.

One simple innovation was to map courses to qualifications, an example being ELITE, the NHS EssentiaL IT skills course, certified by the British Computer Society. Julie describes her team's delivery of the course as "incredibly blended, but all within a classroom. Learners were always discovering things, constantly being challenged and excited." The qualification was a big draw, attracting people who had previously avoided IT. However, staff could also take the ELITE qualification by e-learning with tutor support by phone and email. This was a major change that was a big hit with community-based healthcare workers who found it difficult to take a full day out for training.

Subsequent qualification-based courses that were pure e-learning also had a huge uptake. Anyone who enrolled in e-learning was assigned a tutor who kept in touch with them by phone and kept them on track. The fact that they knew they were being monitored was an important source of motivation. The successful adoption of e-learning as an accepted method of delivering training proved to be vital during the swine flu epidemic in 2009. When the major incident team wanted to provide training to every member of staff, HR's solution was to suggest a series of face-to-face courses. Julie's team offered an e-learning solution which was quickly accepted.

John Turton, Central and Eastern Cheshire PCT Emergency Planning & Business Continuity Manager, had this to say: "From a basic outline of requirement, which changed daily as more national data was received, the team produced three initial pieces of e-learning that still stand good today, saving hours of training time and hitting the whole organisation."

Julie started getting the good news stories out in the form of case studies and news bites. The team changed the way they delivered the ICT section of the Acute Trust's junior doctors' induction, including the provision of software simulations and e-learning to stop the previous practice of teaching new doctors very hurriedly on live data. This e-learning was accessible via the junior doctors' mobile devices, providing them with access to the training they need 24/7. Julie describes how the new approach did a much better job: "The doctors could work at their own pace whenever they had down time. This was very much just-in-time learning. " A bi-product of creating this e-learning was that it could also be used by other professionals that needed to understand and use the same healthcare systems.

The team was clearly starting to align itself to the business, as Wendy Barker, PGME Support Manager Education, attested: "We have worked closely with the training team over the last year and have always found them to be helpful and supportive. I feel the team works collaboratively with us so that we understand where we are each coming from and what we want to jointly achieve."

Thinking synchronous

Next in line was to introduce synchronous online learning. With no budget, Julie took out a free 30-day trial of Adobe Connect and cheekily kept extending it. Julie explained, "We wanted to use virtual classrooms because a lot of people would not come on a full or half-day course – particularly if they only needed a bit or a recap or a top-up. We ran half-hour sessions on topics like email etiquette, better internet searching, or managing your inbox better. It helped that they didn't have to get formal approval to attend because the sessions were so short."

The team kept the groups small and adopted a very relaxed style, using discussion, Q&A and the sharing of screens. The aim was to take learners on to the next stage where they could continue the discussion in forums within SharePoint. Here they could also access short screencasts created using the free software tool Jing.

Julie admits she had no money to obtain Oracle's performance support system (Oracle systems are heavily used in the NHS) but would have loved it. Instead they gave out very simple 'how do I?' booklets, which were also made available as PDFs on SharePoint. The booklets did not cover every aspect of every system, but concentrated on those tasks that learners most needed to know about and where the business benefit was greatest.

All's well ...

The leverage that Julie needed to really influence management came when they won awards from the Institute of IT Training for Internal Project of the Year and, most significantly, for Internal Training Department of the Year. To emphasise the point they won this again a year later. Needless to say, the money for Adobe Connect was soon forthcoming.

The training team has continued to provide an outstanding professional service to all manner of customers from across the Cheshire ICT Service footprint within Cheshire. The team continued to push the boundaries by embracing and delivering an innovative and creative service flexing to the needs of different organisations.

Stuart Lea, Associate Director CICTS, summarises well: "The team has opened my eyes to how users can learn both at a pace and in a style that suits them. We used to work in old-fashioned ways which I would not like to go back to. The training team are very much of the moment and continually looking to improve and move with the times."

Julie has over 25 years' experience of teaching and training across a wide range of industry sectors in the UK, Europe and the USA. With a particular focus on IT-related learning and change management, Julie specialises in the practical application of learning technologies in the real world, helping organisations, trainers and learners to learn and work smarter.

Julie is a Fellow of the Institute of IT Training and is a member of the Institute of IT Training Advisory Board. She regularly presents at conferences and events, both in the UK and globally online.

Non-formal learning

We continue our tour of the contextual model with a look at non-formal learning. In a way we've already started, because both formal learning, which we reviewed in the last chapter, and non-formal learning are proactive approaches. Formal learning stands apart because it packages up the learning intervention in the guise of a 'course', with clearly established objectives, curriculum and assessment. In this chapter we look at the myriad of interventions which are much less formal, but still make a major contribution to learning and development in the workplace.

To refresh your memory, non-formal learning as we define it here is 'learning to' with a future perspective. It is not concerned with 'learning from' what we have done in the past, nor 'learning to' do something right now to address an immediate need. It occurs whenever we take deliberate steps to prepare ourselves for the tasks that we will be carrying out in the future or when others do this on our behalf. Some cynics label it 'just-in-case' learning, in contrast to learning that takes place 'just-in-time'. Non-formal learning takes many shapes, but stops short of those interventions packaged up as formal courses.

The argument for proactive approaches

Proactive approaches, formal or non-formal, are important because there are certain fundamental things we need to know and skills we need to have before we can make any serious attempt to function in our present jobs, or take on new responsibilities:

Induction and basic training: We are recruited as much as anything for the skills and knowledge we already possess, for our years of experience with other employers and for our qualifications. But every employer is different in terms of their culture, their particular policies and procedures, and the people that they employ. Even the most qualified new recruit requires some induction whereas, at the other end of the scale, many starters require weeks, months or even years of basic training.

Business change: Only rarely do jobs remain static – responsibilities change along with new strategies, processes and systems, creating new requirements for knowledge and skill.

Development: Looking ahead, organisations and employees themselves have an obvious interest in making preparations for employees to take on greater responsibilities.

So why not on-demand learning?

On-demand learning is just-in-time performance support – it's there when you need it. But, although performance support has many advantages, it is not a panacea. Alison Rossett and Lisa Schafer[52] have identified four situations in which you need to have the knowledge and skills *before* you undertake the task:

When aided performance would damage credibility: There are times when you would look amateurish if you had to go seeking out information that others might expect you to know. The obvious example is when you are dealing directly with customers or clients. No-one's going to be bothered if you have to obtain help to deal with an unusual situation, but they would be justifiably annoyed if, say, you were a sales assistant in a retail store and couldn't operate the till, or were an electrician who couldn't wire a plug.

---

[52] *Job Aids & Performance Support* by Alison Rossett & Lisa Schafer, Pfeiffer, 2007.

When speedy performance is a priority: In some jobs, there simply isn't the time to go tracking down the right information or asking for help. A lawyer may have time to consult the books, but an airline pilot needs to be able to respond to an emergency using their own resources; a business person may be able to consult with a specialist before determining a strategy, but a professional sportsperson has to be able to swiftly select the right tactics to deal with a situation that arises unexpectedly.

When novel and unpredictable situations are involved: Some jobs are relatively stable and it may be possible for an employer to prepare performance support materials or systems to cope with every eventuality. Many other jobs are much less predictable and it is vital for the employee to be equipped with the core skills and problem-solving strategies to deal with the unexpected when it occurs. Take the example of an investment banker: although much of their work might be routine, they have to be able to deal swiftly with crisis situations that sometimes have no precedence.

When smooth and fluid performance is a top priority: Performance support is disruptive – it interrupts the task and disturbs the flow. No audience is going to wait while a presenter consults Wikipedia to look up a fact or asks for help in operating PowerPoint; similarly a telephone sales representative will not want to keep the customer waiting while they consult with a colleague.

Then why not formal learning?

We've already argued the case for formal learning, but it should be clear that, although running a course can often be the right way to address a need, there are many more cases where an alternative will be more effective and more efficient. Back in 1970, Peter

Honey[53] pleaded for us to 'stop the courses, I want to get off.' He argued that organising courses was the easy option, but that to create effective learning situations which were meaningful in terms of the job called for much more effort, imagination and innovation.

Nearly forty years later, Donald Clark[54] took up where Peter Honey left off: "Maslow's hierarchy of needs, that great staple of train the trainer courses, is typical of the simplistic junk that is thrown about in the training world, but he did have one great line: 'If you walk around long enough with a hammer, everything starts to look like a nail'. That's training, folks. Our hammer is the 'course' – the pat solution for every problem."

He elaborated as follows: "Courses are also at odds with the psychology of learning. We know that 'spaced practice' is a necessary condition for almost all learning, yet almost all courses do the opposite, delivering large, single doses. We also know that most skills need a 'learn by doing' approach, yet most courses are skewed towards knowledge. We know that learning is about long-term memory, yet most courses focus on short-term memory and assessment. We know that learning needs to avoid cognitive overload, yet most courses suffer from an obesity of content. We know that learning benefits from being situated in the context in which the learning is to be put to use, yet most courses pluck people out of this context. I could go on and on, but perhaps the greatest problem is the sheer lack of knowledge and awareness of the basics of the psychology of learning, and its application in training. It's like engineers who build bridges but know nothing about physics."

---

[53] *Stop the courses! I want to get off* by Peter Honey, Industrial and Commercial Training, Volume 2, Issue 5, 1970.
[54] *Stop the courses, I want to get off* by Donald Clark, TrainingZone, March 2009.

Perhaps, if you'll excuse the pun, it's just a case of horses for courses. There are many good reasons why some learning should be formal, why some should be conducted in groups, why some courses should be carried out in real-time as opposed to being self-paced, and why some should be face-to-face as opposed to online. And there are equally good reasons for doing the opposite. In the end the choices you make should be made on the basis of the particular situation, not familiarity, prejudice or predisposition. And if that choice is made well, effectiveness will then depend on how well you carry the job out.

Top-down approaches

Employers have a wide range of non-formal options at their disposal that they can implement on a top-down basis:

On-job training

On-job training is the original and probably still the most common way of getting employees up-to-scratch in their new jobs. Because of its relative informality, it is often looked down on as an inferior option, merely 'sitting next to Nellie', yet it's an enduring favourite with employees themselves. True, it does have its drawbacks:

- The quality depends a great deal on the skills of the person doing the instructing.
- There's no guarantee that the instructor will convey the official 'company line'.
- The learner does not get to interact with their peers.
- The instructor is unlikely to have had the time to prepare anything but the most rudimentary visual aids or handouts.
- The 1:1 teacher student ratio is expensive.

But the benefits are significant enough to be worth hanging on to:

- The instruction is highly personalised.
- The on-job setting maximises transfer of learning.
- The learner gets to practice in an authentic work setting.
- The instruction is likely to be practical, relevant and up-to-date.

And employees do like on-job training, as explained in a 2008 report from the Chartered Institute of Personnel and Development[55]: "Individual preferences are for social rather than solitary learning. The unequivocal preferred method is for being shown how to do things and being given the opportunity to practise. On-the-job training is the preferred method of learning for all categories of employee. This can be seen as a mismatch to the amount of classroom-based learning that is taking place."

Employees realise that practice makes perfect, but their teachers don't always appreciate this. As Seely Brown and Duquid[56] make clear: "The idea of learning as the steady supply of facts and information, though parodied by Dickens 150 years ago, still prevails today. Each generation has to fight its own battle against images of learners as wax to be moulded, pitchers to be filled, and slates to be written on." To 'know that' is not to 'know how'; 'learning about' something does not necessarily equip you to 'learn to be' the person who successfully carries out a particular job role. "Information is not enough to produce actionable knowledge. Practice too is required."

---

[55] *Supporting, accelerating and directing learning* from the Chartered Institute of Personnel and Development (CIPD), 2008

[56] *The Social Life of Information* by John Seely Brown and Paul Duquid, Harvard Business School Press, 2002.

Jay Cross[57] asks who is going to provide all this on-job training: "Now that business organizations have been de-layered, downsized, and re-engineered to the bone, how will they transfer their special ways of doing things to new employees? The answer lies in exploiting the savvy of seniors, the wise elders who have 'been there, done that' and can offer counsel and know-how to the newcomers." But wise elders are in short supply, and prone to what Chip and Dan Heath[58] call the 'curse of knowledge' – the tendency that most experts have to believe that others have the same knowledge and interests as they do and are therefore as fascinated by the theory, the abstractions and the detail of their jobs. The answer is to assign the task of on-job training to those qualified not only in terms of their job experience but also their ability to empathise with the learner.

Some useful tips are provided by Steve Trautman[59] in his book *Teach what you know*. He recommends a sensible sequence for the instruction, starting with the 'air, food and water', i.e. the basics needed for survival in the job, moving on to give the big picture, then the skills. He encourages the use of questions, before, during and after the instruction, to assess needs and check understanding. He understands the problems of cognitive overload and recommends providing the "least amount of information necessary to make the employee successful at the task." He understands the problems of transfer and knows how to overcome this through the use of worked examples and practical exercises.

Apprenticeship is a special form of on-job training. According to the Wikipedia, "apprenticeship is a system of training a new generation

---

[57] *Learning is strictly business* by Jay Cross, 2007
[58] *Made to Stick* by Chip Heath and Dan Heath, Random House, 2007
[59] *Teach what you know* by Steve Trautman, Prentice Hall, 2007

of practitioners of a skill." Most of this training is conducted on-the-job while the apprentice works for an employer who helps them to learn their trade, in exchange for their continuing labour for an agreed period after they become skilled. Apprenticeships have a long tradition in the United Kingdom, dating back to around the 12th century and flourishing by the 14th century. A master craftsman was entitled to employ young people as an inexpensive form of labour in exchange for providing formal training in the craft.

Modern apprenticeships tend to include a knowledge-based element, often provided through part-time formal study, and a skills element provided on-job. The scope of apprenticeships has also widened to include occupations outside the traditional crafts. For the trainee, an apprenticeship provides the opportunity to gain skills and knowledge on-the-job and to work towards a qualification while earning. For the employer, apprenticeships help employers to develop the next generation of skilled workers in partnership with the government and the education sector.

On-job training is:

- *at its best when* conducted by trained instructors, highly practical, personalised to the individual learner;
- *best avoided when* focused on knowledge transfer, poorly structured, does no more than throw the learner in at the deep end.

Coaching

While on-job training is focused primarily on the provision of the basic skills needed for an employee to learn a new job, coaching is very much a developmental activity. To take a very obvious sporting example, top athletes such as tennis players and footballers receive continuous coaching throughout their careers, often from coaches who are not capable of performing at the level of their coachees. It is taken for granted that performance can always be improved and that the chances of this improvement taking place will be much enhanced if the performer's own efforts are supported by a coach.

According to the CIPD's Learning and Development Survey for 2008, the majority of coaching is undertaken for general personal development or as part of a wider management and leadership development programme. However, a significant amount of coaching also takes place to remedy problem behaviour or to bring about a specific change in performance. Typically the objectives for this coaching are determined for the individual coachee, rather than on the basis of a wider company programme. The bulk of the responsibility for coaching lies with line managers, although it is not uncommon for organisations to employee dedicated internal or external coaches.

There are many models for performance coaching in organisations, but most focus on helping the coachee to analyse and solve their own challenges, rather than offering advice or direction. A commonly used model for this process is GROW:

G is for Goal: What do you really want?

R is for Reality: Identify where you are and what you have.

O is for Obstacles: What is stopping you achieving your goals.

O is also for Options: Exploring alternative ways forward.

W is for Way Forward: Creating your action plan, and getting started.

Business coaching is not the same as mentoring. Mentoring involves a developmental relationship between a more experienced mentor and a less experienced partner, and typically involves the sharing of advice. A business coach can act also as a mentor if they have adequate expertise and experience, but the mentoring and coaching are separate processes.

Coaching is:

- *at its best when* goal-focused, orientated around real work issues, non-directive, aimed at developing the coachee's confidence;
- *best avoided when* simply going through the motions, when not followed through, when encourages dependence on the coach.

Webinars

A webinar is essentially an online seminar, conducted using web conferencing technology. Web conferencing systems vary to some extent, but most have the following capabilities:

- Two-way audio either through an accompanying teleconference, or online using Voice Over internet Protocol (VOIP). The latter is much less expensive, but does require the user's PC to have audio capability and for reasonable bandwidth to be available.
- The ability to present slides, typically imported from PowerPoint.
- A 'virtual whiteboard' facility, allowing presenters and users to type or draw on a common visual space.
- The ability to share any user's desktop and any applications running on the user's computer.

- A text chat facility, allowing users to ask or respond to questions, and to send messages to each other.

- The ability to jointly view material on a website.

- The ability to make a recording of a session for use by those who were unable to attend or who need a recap.

- A polling/survey facility.

- The ability to see the presenter and, perhaps, selected participants, using an online video feed. This feature will undoubtedly become more common as bandwidth increases.

A webinar suffers in comparison with a face-to-face event because of its limited capability to allow participants to see each other, particularly where online video is not available. However, there are other ways in which a webinar might be the preferred option:

- When it is impractical for participants to travel to a central location.

- When it would be too costly or time-consuming to bring a specialist presenter to a face-to-face event.

- When it is important that the event is recorded and made available for viewing subsequently.

A typical webinar lasts between 45 and 90 minutes. Longer programmes are possible, but should be broken up into a series of shorter sessions.

Webinars are:

- *at their best when* the sessions are relatively short, are well supported by visuals and highly interactive;

- *best avoided when* endless PowerPoint, monotone speakers, no participation.

Podcasts

Podcasts provide a new way to package up audio recordings for learning purposes. While tapes and CDs do provide reasonable sound quality, they are difficult and expensive to duplicate and distribute, whereas podcasts need only to be edited, converted to MP3 format and then distributed online.

While a single podcast can be easily accessed online for playback on a PC or Mac, the real power comes when you distribute your podcasts using a subscription service through software such as Apple's iTunes. The software will then automatically download each new 'episode' as it comes available and, if required, copy this to the user's iPod or similar portable MP3 player. The next time the user is out and about, perhaps commuting to work or on a business trip, they will be able to listen to the latest podcast without having to be involved in any way in the mechanics of download and transfer.

However sexy the technology, a podcast is still just an audio file, limited in content to speech, music and sound effects, and without any in-built facility for interaction. Having said that, audio material can undoubtedly make a contribution to the on-going learning process, particularly when used as part of a broader programme of interventions. Podcasts are particularly well suited to interviews and panel discussions, which tend to be much more compelling to listen to than monologues. If in doubt, try to copy the techniques used on radio programmes, which rarely rely on a single voice.

Podcasts are:

- *at their best when* they use an interview or discussion format, are not tightly scripted, are kept short or divided into several short sections;
- *best avoided when* restricted to a single voice, when that voice is monotone, when over-long.

White papers

According to the Wikipedia, a white paper is "an authoritative report or guide that often addresses problems and how to solve them. White papers are used to educate readers and help people make decisions." Organisations can use white papers to explore any issue that is of current performance and to disseminate the results widely amongst internal and external audiences. Typically the papers will be written by experts or those who have conducted in-depth research into particular topics, and then distributed as printed documents, PDFs or as web pages.

A library of white papers provides a useful resource to support non-formal learning, particularly for knowledge workers who need access to in-depth analysis of current topics. The best results will be achieved alongside other media and more interactive approaches, including rapid e-learning content, short workshops, webinars, podcasts and online discussions.

White papers are:

- *at their best when* they are clear and to the point, supported by appropriate charts and diagrams, written at the right level for the intended audience and supported by opportunities for discussion;

- *best avoided when* lengthy and complex, written in over-formal language, poorly formatted.

Mini workshops

Mini workshops provide developmental training in short bursts, often over a lunchtime. Along with the growth of rapid e-learning, they demonstrate how tight learning time now is in most organisations and how l&d departments must be increasingly flexible and imaginative in their responses to needs.

Short workshops need to be tightly focused, typically on a single topic. If they are not, content delivery will crowd out Q&A, discussion and practical work, and participants might find they would be better off listening to a recording.

They also need to be well promoted, as one organisation reported as part of research conducted by SkillSoft in 2007[60]: "Short one and two hour sessions are hugely popular, but they don't just happen. They are very well publicised, with a whole communications package built around them. They are well-promoted and are pushed through the organisation using intranet, messenger and email. Line managers are involved too – telling people how they can benefit from doing the learning."

Mini workshops are

- *at their best when* limited to a single topic, lively and interactive and highly relevant to real-work issues;
- *best avoided when* no more than a lecture, abstract and theoretical.

---

[60] *The Future of Learning*, SkillSoft, 2007

Rapid e-learning

Rapid e-learning is a form of self-paced e-learning content that is developed quickly and intended to be accessed in short chunks and outside the context of a formalised intervention. Bersin and Associates define rapid e-learning as "web-based training programmes that can be created in a few weeks and which are authored largely by subject-matter experts," although in practice the content is as likely to be developed by generalist trainers or external contractors, and could just as easily be assembled in days or even hours. The pressure is certainly on for more rapid responses to learning needs. According to a report by Bersin in 2005, "78% of trainers in the US are under pressure to develop e-learning more rapidly." In the same year the eLearning Guild found that "72% of all training challenges are time-critical."

If rapid e-learning is to live up to its name it requires easy-to-use tools and streamlined processes. Two types of tools have emerged to fill this need:

- **PowerPoint-based tools**: with these, much of the layout and structuring of the material is accomplished in the familiar PowerPoint interface; the material can then be extended to include narrations, quizzes, surveys and other interactions, and converted to Flash for delivery online. Examples include Articulate and Adobe Presenter.

- **Software training tools**: these make it possible to record software operations as movies that faithfully demonstrate every mouse movement and menu selection; the movies can be enriched with labels, explanations, questions and exercises, before conversion to Flash for deployment online. Examples include Adobe Captivate and Techsmith Camtasia.

Typical formal e-learning development processes are too cumbersome for situations requiring a rapid response. As Jay Cross[61] explains, "Time trumps perfection. In the old days, training wasn't released until it passed through a gauntlet of editors, proof-readers, packagers, double-checkers, and worry-warts — lots of training was obsolete before it hit the street. The net has taught us to value timeliness over relentless typo searching. Everything is a work in progress. If it's not finished, label it DRAFT or Beta, but don't hold it up. Think of a blog: part of its charm is its informality, the idiosyncrasies of its author, and its status as an opinion, not a law. People learn more when presented with material that is controversial because uncertainty engages the mind."

So, although some planning is essential, the key with a rapid process is to get a product up as quickly as possible and to get this in front of real users. The product can then be continuously refined until it meets the needs precisely.

Where the rapid materials are explicitly instructional, they should incorporate the interactive elements necessary to ensure learning takes place. Alternatively they can be kept as simple expositions and used in conjunction with other, more interactive approaches such as short workshops, webinars or online discussions.

Good tools do not guarantee good content and so inexperienced e-learning developers will need some training. Recognising this, a number of experienced designers from around the world co-operated in 2007 in the development of the '60-minute masters[62],' a course for training part-time authors. They recommended the following as the basis for the curriculum:

---

[61] Ibid

[62] *The 60-minute Masters* wiki is no longer available. An implementation of the course can be found at http://onlignment.com/the-60-minute-masters/

Prepare

Set a realistic goal

Consider the content from the learner's point of view

Inform

Hook learners in emotionally

Present your material clearly, simply and in a logical order

Illuminate your material with imagery

Use audio appropriately

Consolidate

Put your material into context with examples, cases and stories

Engage users with challenging interactions

End with a call to action

Rapid e-learning materials are:

- *at their best when* relevant, quick and simple, engaging and well supported by visuals;

- *best avoided when* abstract, over-long, too detailed and overly textual.

Internal conferences

An organisation's internal conferences are not usually thought of as learning events, but they often constitute the primary means for employees to stay up-to-date with developments within the organisation. Importantly, they also provide a valuable opportunity for reflection, discussion and networking. Conferences are highly expensive events to stage, not only in terms of the preparation involved, but also travel and subsistence expenses, not to mention lost work time. To take advantage of the opportunities provided and to justify the expenditure, every conference needs to be carefully planned.

It is important not to waste the opportunity of having all the players that work in a particular function or at a particular management level present, face-to-face at the same time. Presentations can be useful if they allow senior managers and subject experts to convey important messages engagingly and succinctly, and to stimulate discussion, problem-solving and decision-making. What they must not do is dominate the timetable, because in the end they are just another form of one-way communication and other, more practical, means exist for this purpose, not least audio, video, the Intranet and print. As Samuel Johnson (1709-1784) explained long ago: "Lectures were once useful; but now, when all can read, and books are so numerous, lectures are unnecessary. If your attention fails, and you miss a part of a lecture, it is lost; you cannot go back as you do upon a book..."

Three hundred years later, the situation is much the same, as Donald Clark[63] laments: "Conferences are mirror images of the classroom. By and large people turn up to be spoon-fed by sages on the stage talking at them, with the occasional opportunity to ask questions. It has one, and only one, advantage over the classroom – scale. It's a lazy approach to learning made even more inefficient by the fact that even learning professionals often fail to take notes. This makes it a forgetting experience. The best one can hope for, as a speaker, is to affect some emotional or attitudinal shift. And when people get back to the ranch they rarely write up their findings and distribute them across the organisation. If one were to truly apply a ROI justification for conference attendance, few would be able to look you in the eye."

---

[63] *Conferences – jumped up classrooms?* by Donald Clark, Plan B, November 2008 at http://donaldclarkplanb.blogspot.com/2008/11/conferences-jumped-up-classrooms.html

Real value comes from the interactions that occur between those peers that in other circumstances meet only rarely, without interruptions and other distractions, and hopefully without the constraints normally imposed by hierarchy. Much of this will occur naturally, between formal sessions, but this is wasting too much of the opportunity. Be sure to provide focused problem-solving sessions, debates and discussions, as a formal part of the agenda.

Internal conferences are:

- *at their best when* lively and interactive, highly relevant, varied, primarily bottom-up but with some inspiring top-down input;
- *best avoided when* lengthy, monotonous, presentation-driven, entirely top-down.

Online video

Time was when 'corporate video' was commonplace, at least in larger organisations. In the 1980s many employers established their own in-house video studios to develop a constant stream of communications and training programmes for distribution on their dedicated VHS video networks. Others made use of external production companies and were happy to pay at least £1000 per finished minute for the privilege. It is commonly thought that the main driver behind the growth of corporate video was the proliferation of low-cost VCRs in the home – managers realised the potential of video by using it for themselves.

The shift towards digital media in the 1990s rather left analogue video behind. CD-ROM was a more interactive, versatile and easily-distributed medium, although it was far too slow in the early days to handle video in anything other than the tiniest windows. By the time CD-ROMs had increased sufficiently in speed to cope with video, the in-house video units had been disbanded and the whole idea lost. When, at the end of the 1990s, technology shifted again towards online delivery, bandwidth restrictions kept video very much on the backburner.

Well, video has returned and with a vengeance. Bandwidth is now much less of an issue and it is incomparably cheaper than it was in the 1980s to produce video – low-cost cameras and easy-to-use PC-based editing software have taken much of the mystery out of video production. But it is the fantastic success of YouTube which has done the most to bring online video into the public consciousness. Now many organisations are seeking to emulate YouTube behind the firewall by establishing their own video channels, often with Web 2.0 characteristics, including the tagging of content, commenting and rating on content by viewers and – in some cases – the uploading of new videos to the library by any user.

Video is a powerful medium which is capable of attracting and holding attention more powerfully than text, audio or still images. As long as the content is relevant and clearly communicated there is no need for high production values. YouTube has emphasised once again that fitness for purpose is the only true test of quality.

Online video is:

- *at its best when* delivered in short chunks, highly relevant, visually varied, the audio is of good quality;
- *best avoided when* too static, over-long, with poor audio, monotone delivery.

Bottom-up approaches

There may well be a plethora of opportunities available for top-down non-formal learning, but there's still plenty of scope for bottom-up initiatives:

Open learning

Open learning gives the learner flexibility and choice over what, when, at what pace, where, and how they learn. It is normally associated with self-study, using a variety of media including books, workbooks, CD-ROMs and online materials. Much open learning is carried out at a distance, in many cases from home, but can also be based in a learning centre at a college or on an employer's premises.

Open learning materials are typically structured into courses, but are included here under the non-formal learning heading because they are very often just dipped into, rather than studied in any formal sense. Perhaps the key distinction here is that, although open learning resources may well be made available by the employer, the decision to use them is entirely the employee's. He or she determines what they will study, if anything at all, and to what extent.

Open learning resources are funded by employers because they provide a simple and inexpensive way to encourage and support employee self-development. Libraries of off-the-shelf self-study materials can typically be purchased or licensed at relatively low per-user prices and require little in the way of back up. However, if the open learning is seen as no more than a peripheral employee benefit, there is a good chance that the facility will not be used to anything near its capacity.

Open learning is:

- *at its best when* it forms an integral part of the l&d strategy, is supported by line managers, is available as short modules, is lightly structured, uses high-quality materials;
- *best avoided when* peripheral, unsupported, low in quality.

Continuing professional development

Many employees belong to a profession of some sort, whether that is function-specific – such as marketing, HR, software engineering, accounting, teaching and so on – or generic, such as management. Some of these professions require their members to undertake some form of continuing professional development (CPD) as a condition of membership; others simply encourage this.

Resources for CPD can originate from professional bodies, but also from commercial providers such as publishers and conference organisers. Those employees who identify with a particular profession are likely to have a wide range of resources to choose from:

- Magazines and journals
- Conferences and webinars
- Meetings of regional groups, chapters, working parties, etc.
- Books, videos, podcasts and other media resources

It is impractical for all but the largest organisations to provide CPD resources internally. There is also a strong argument for actively encouraging external CPD events and resources as a means for learning what other organisations are doing and benchmarking one's own organisation against the best in class.

Continuing professional development is:

- *at its best when* the resources are engaging and relevant, when the outcomes are shared with other professionals in the same organisation, when integrated into an employee's development plan;

- *best avoided when* participants are just doing it because they have to, when the resources are paid for but never used.

Communities of practice

Whether or not an employee is a member of anything as formal as a professional association, they almost certainly belong to a body of practitioners of a particular skill or trade. These bodies can be formalised either within an organisation or more broadly across a country or region as a community of practice. The benefits are profound, as Seely Brown and Duquid[64] make clear: "In learning to be, in becoming a member of a community of practice, an individual is developing a social identity."

Peter Henschel[65], formerly of the Institute for Research on Learning, and a keen proponent of social learning, famously set out these seven principles:

1. Learning is fundamentally social. While learning is about the process of acquiring knowledge, it actually encompasses a lot more. Successful learning is often socially constructed and can require slight changes in one's identity, which makes the process both challenging and powerful.

---

[64] Ibid
[65] *Report from the Future: Sustaining Innovation and Continuous Improvement* by Peter Henschel, Institute for Research on Learning

2. Knowledge is integrated in the life of communities. When we develop and share values, perspectives, and ways of doing things, we create a community of practice.

3. Learning is an act of participation. The motivation to learn is the desire to participate in a community of practice, to become and remain a member. This is a key dynamic that helps explain the power of apprenticeship and the attendant tools of mentoring and peer coaching.

4. Knowing depends on engagement in practice. We often glean knowledge from observation of, and participation in, many different situations and activities. The depth of our knowing depends, in turn, on the depth of our engagement.

5. Engagement is inseparable from empowerment. We perceive our identities in terms of our ability to contribute and to affect the life of communities in which we are or want to be a part.

6. Failure to learn is often the result of exclusion from participation. Learning requires access and the opportunity to contribute.

7. We are all natural lifelong learners. All of us, no exceptions. Learning is a natural part of being human. We all learn what enables us to participate in the communities of practice of which we wish to be a part.

Outside the workplace, it has become ever easier for people with common interests to form online communities, whether informally, through some type of online groups facility (as provided free by Microsoft, Yahoo!, Google and others) or, more recently, using social networking sites like Facebook or LinkedIn. While it is unrealistic to expect employers to make use of sites which are primarily intended for personal use, many social networking ideas can be borrowed for use in enterprise systems:

- Establishing an online profile.

- Forming relationships with other users of the site who have similar interests or requirements in order to create your own personal network.

- Sharing news, thoughts, links with others in your network.

- Contributing resources (documents, presentations, videos, podcasts) which other members of your network might find useful.

- Adding tags (descriptive labels) to resources, so they can be easily found by others.

- Rating and commenting on the resources of others.

These activities are now so commonplace outside the workplace that employees will increasingly become frustrated when they are denied the same opportunities at work. In high-tech companies, they will not be disappointed: according to John Chambers, the CEO of Cisco, the firm saved $150 million through collaborative tools that harnessed networks of ideas. "For the first time, collaborative IT will be so intertwined with the business strategy, you won't know the difference between the two," he said.

Bradwell and Reeves[66] emphasise the new importance of networking: "Humans are social animals, spinning intricate webs of relationships with friends, colleagues, neighbours and enemies. These networks have always been with us, but the advance of networking technologies, changes to our interconnected economy

---

[66] *Network Citizens: Power and Responsibility at Work* by Peter Bradwell and Richard Reeves, DEMOS, 2008, http://www.demos.co.uk/publications/networkcitizens

and an altering job market have super-charged the power of networking, catapulting it to the heart of organisational thinking."

Communities of practice are:

- *at their best when* they come together naturally, when members share freely, when democratic, open and responsive;
- *best avoided when* artificial and contrived, hierarchical, conservative.

Conditions for success

To enjoy success, it is important for the l&d professional to recognise that:

- learning needs to be continuous throughout employees' careers;
- not all learning needs to be packaged as formal courses, because more informal approaches are often perfectly adequate;
- many, short inputs will have more impact than a few lengthy ones;
- many players can contribute to the provision of learning experiences and materials, not just learning and development professionals;
- skills in the development and provision of learning experiences and materials should be widely distributed within the organisation.

Profile: Tiina Paju-Pomfret

In this next profile, we see another fine example of how a learning and development department has been able to break free from the confines of the face-to-face course to provide support for learning across multiple contexts.

Rethinking formal ICT training

Working alongside colleague Kerry Baker, Tiina has transformed ICT training at Bupa. The old model of lengthy, face-to-face, instructor-led courses was failing to appeal to the next generation of learners who Tiina recognised had shorter attention spans.

Tiina, together with her team of experienced trainers, established a new blended training model combining instructor-led training with self-study e-learning and support by telephone and email. A portfolio of learning assets was created, which included 'above the line' learning interventions (instructor-led classroom and online classroom) as well as 'below the line' (e-learning, email and phone support, with corporate social networking groups).

All members of the team were trained to adapt their skills to working in the virtual classroom and they have now devised their own distinct methodology for delivering tight, 1-2 hour sessions. This was accomplished using Bupa's Saba Centra virtual classroom platform.

The team still delivers some one day, face-to-face courses, but with a shift in emphasis away from simply teaching software applications towards focusing on how those applications can be used to help you work more effectively. A good example would be Bupa's course on time management using Outlook.

Community and collaboration

Working alongside the new blended learning offering sits a powerful community, collaboration and social media platform called *Bupa Live*, which is based on Jive SBS software. *Bupa Live* originated as a business project at the very top of the organisation, with the aim of 'creating one Bupa' across the global business. Starting from a small pilot of around 1000 employees, usage grew virally and currently some 10,000 employees are users. Perhaps the most used feature of the system is the discussion forum, although there is a top-down element as well through corporate blogs, news and videos. In addition, Bupa Live used to support communication amongst groups, a facility that has been used heavily as the IT community has shifted to a more agile development process.

Bupa Live also acts as a first port of call in Tiina's strategy for on-demand learning: "We like employees to use this platform, perhaps posing a question to one of the forums. If needs be, employees can ring the IS Service Centre or one of the trainers." The team also uses Bupa Live for more informal training needs analysis to gather requirements directly from the learner audience.

Bupa Live acts as a valuable repository for more informal learning resources, but direct links can easily be made to *Bupa Learn*, the Saba-based LMS. As Tiina says, "It's all about making things easy for our learners."

Agile course development

Tiina has adopted agile frameworks for her own team's development projects. Using techniques borrowed from user-centred design, the team created personas of their key target groups and looks to ensure that every aspect of the design supports their needs. For each persona they develop 'user stories' which express in the everyday or business language of the user what it is that the user wants to achieve. These stories then form the basis for the modules of the course. The team are able to create courses quicker using a collaborative approach whilst maintaining quality. As Tiina says, "It works!

In many cases the solution that the team will arrive at will be e-learning, which they produce in house using tools such as Captivate and Lectora. Increasingly the team is looking to create small nuggets no more than 5-15 minutes in length. Production values play second fiddle to simplicity and effectiveness. As Tiina explains, "It doesn't have to be perfect and polished – it just has to do a good job."

Tiina is an experienced and forward-thinking learning and development professional with a career in training and consulting that has covered a wide range of business sectors. She brings a strong level of innovation, creativity and passion for learning using a variety of methodologies.

Tiina is currently training manager in the Business Technology Training department at Bupa, an international healthcare group with over 10 million customers in more than 190 countries. The department was set up ten years ago to ensure the quality of ICT skills across Bupa's diverse workforce. Since Tiina took over the department in 2005, she has overseen some impressive changes.

On-demand learning

We move on to look at the third element in the contextual model, on-demand learning. To refresh our memories, on-demand learning is a form of 'learning to'. It occurs because we don't know how to perform a particular task and therefore need immediate help to acquire the necessary knowledge. To use more familiar terminology, on-demand learning can be regarded as 'just-in-time learning' or 'learning at the point of need'.

Some would argue that on-demand learning isn't learning at all, because the objective is to support performance not to teach. There's no guarantee, indeed there may be no real concern, that an employee acquires in any permanent way the knowledge needed to carry out the task, just so long as they can do it right now. After all, a task may only ever need to be carried out once or only so occasionally that the effort required to retain the knowledge may not be justifiable.

However, there's a very blurry line between just-in-time performance support and long-term learning. The information itself is likely to be the same; the same people may be approached to provide this information; the same materials may be used in each case. The main difference comes with the strategy:

- When the goal is performance, the information must be available at the point of need for easy reference.
- When the goal is learning (a more or less permanent set of new connections in the brain), the intervention must go beyond providing information to include practice, assessment and feedback.

L&d professionals may argue that it is not their role to provide reference information. There may even be a completely independent team responsible for technical documentation. But this argument doesn't stand up to close analysis:

- Trainers have always contributed to the provision of reference material through the handouts and job aids that they provide with their classroom courses.

- Technical documentation may be an option of last resort, but is unlikely to be a user-friendly and easily-accessible resource that does the job on a day-to-day basis.

- The fact that much of the same content is required for both training and for performance support makes it uneconomic to develop separately.

- L&d professionals are uniquely well equipped to present information clearly and simply.

Another way to reconcile the concept of performance support with learning is to conceive that knowledge can exist beyond the individual, in their own personal network of digital and human connections. The idea of the 'outboard brain' is closely associated with a new theoretical perspective to learning called *connectivism*, as developed by George Siemens[67]:

"Instead of the individual having to evaluate and process every bit of information, she/he creates a personal network of trusted nodes: people and content, enhanced by technology. The act of knowledge is offloaded onto the network itself."

Connectivism places new demands on the l&d professional who, as a facilitator of learning networks, should help to provide the

[67] *Knowing Knowledge* by George Siemens, 2006

infrastructure that enables employees to more easily make connections with sources of expertise. Underpinning this role is a realisation that "the connections that enable us to learn more are more important than our current state of knowing. 'Knowing where' and 'knowing who' are more important today than knowing when and how."

As Jay Cross[68] reminds us, "Successful organisations connect people. Learning is social. We learn from, by, and with other people. Conversation, storytelling, and observation are great ways to learn, but they aren't things you do by yourself."

The plight of the knowledge worker

The abundance of information is weighing heavily on the knowledge worker. The statistics are frightening, as Jay Cross[69] reports:

- "In many professions, knowledge workers spend a third of their time looking for answers and helping their colleagues do the same."
- "Only one in five knowledge workers consistently find the information they need to do their jobs."
- "Knowledge workers spend more time recreating existing information they were unaware of than creating original material."

While we're doling out statistics, let's add some more from Charles Jennings[70]:

---

[68] *Learning is strictly business* by Jay Cross, 2007
[69] Ibid

- "The information available to humans is currently growing at a rate of 30% per year. This growth is increasing year on year and showing no sign of slowing."

- "Ninety percent of the new information generated each year is stored on magnetic media of some type."

The message hasn't necessarily got through to the l&d department, as Jennings explains: "Even though we are all aware that we are operating in a world awash with unstructured information, many learning professionals and managers are still obsessed with the task of transferring information into the heads of learners/employees. They, and many of their managers, see that as the end-game of their endeavours."

The inability to find the right information at the right time has a huge cost, as Paul Strassman[71], former VP at Xerox, reports: "Most businesses that are well endowed with technology lose about $5000 a year per workstation on 'stealth spending'. Of this, 22% is for peer support and 30% for the 'futz factor'. The second includes the time users spend in a befuddled state while clearing up unexplained happenings and overcoming the confusion and panic when computers produce enigmatic messages that stop work."

So how do we respond to these pressures? Well, according to John Seely Brown and John Hagel[72]: "Because you don't know what to expect, planning is folly. It's better to be as responsive as possible when the future arrives." That's on-demand learning.

---

[70] *The Point-of-Need: where effective learning really matters* by Charles Jennings, article in Advance series from Saffron Interactive, 2008

[71] Quoted in *The Social Life of Information*, by John Seely Brown and Paul Duquid, Harvard Business School Press, 2002

[72] *The only sustainable edge* by John Seely Brown and John Hagel, Harvard Business School Press, 2005

The argument for on-demand learning

On-demand learning is necessary because, in many jobs, it is impossible to know everything there is to know. And even if, through prolonged study and training, you were lucky enough to get to know it all, you'd soon find that most of it had changed. There's too much to know and it changes far too quickly. In the knowledge economy, it is more important to know where to look – or who to talk to – than it is to have the knowledge yourself.

Alison Rossett and Lisa Schafer[73] have identified a number of situations in which performance support makes particular sense:

When the performance is infrequent: There's no point learning how to carry out a task if you rarely get to perform it, not least because, with insufficient repetitions, the information is unlikely to stick. An example might be setting up a home office network – chances are, you'll only have to do this every 4-5 years, with little reinforcement of the information in between. An exception would be a task that, although carried out rarely, simply has to be carried out proficiently from memory, the most obvious example of which is an emergency procedure.

When the situation is complex, involves many steps or has many attributes: The more complex the task, the less likely you are to be able to remember every important detail. Even if you have been trained formally, performance support materials are a good backup.

---

[73] *Job Aids & Performance Support* by Alison Rossett & Lisa Schafer, Pfeiffer, 2007.

When the consequence of error is intolerable: Highly critical skills may need to be formally developed through intensive training, but when every detail is important, it pays to provide clear instructions at the point-of-need, just to make sure.

When performance depends on knowledge, procedures or approaches that change frequently: There's no point acquiring knowledge which is soon outdated. Take that example of the home office network – five years ago you'd have been laying Ethernet cables, now it's all wireless.

When there is a high turnover and the task is perceived to be simple: It's not only information that's constantly changing, it's people too. In some industries with high employee turnover, there's little point in devoting training time to simple tasks – just provide clear instructions.

When there is little time or few resources to devote to training: In other words, if all else fails, at very least make sure you provide a decent job aid.

Top-down approaches

A number of options exist for organisations to support employees with on-demand learning:

Performance support materials

Performance support is a timeless concept, but a relatively new term. It is a long-standing convention for trainers to provide participants with handouts and other job aids, to help them to recall the key lessons from a course. These provide a friendlier alternative to the procedures manuals which most organisations provide to their employees.

In 1991, Gloria Gery published Electronic Performance Support Systems – a "bold new vision for the modern workplace." She claimed that[74] "We now have the means to provide employee support electronically – and to make it universally and consistently available on demand at any time, in any place, without unnecessary intermediaries."

Gloria was perhaps a little ahead of her time, but there is now no realistic obstacle to the provision of high-quality performance support materials electronically. The reach of these materials has been dramatically increased with developments in mobile devices, which are now capable of providing something approaching desktop computing power in the palm of your hand.

Allison Rossett and Lisa Schafer[75] make a number of useful distinctions between different types of performance support materials:

- Sidekicks or planners
- Stand-alone or embedded support
- Generic or tailored support

Sidekicks are with us in our work, as we act; they are called upon during a challenge. Sidekicks provide information, reminders, directions and warnings, right when they are needed. Sidekicks can be contrasted with **planners**, which are called upon just before or after a challenge. When referred to before performance, they provide information that helps clarify what is to be done or what will happen. When used after performance, they provide

---

[74] *Electronic Performance Support Systems* by Gloria Gery, Ziff Institute, 1991.
[75] Ibid

information to help you reflect on success and plan for future adjustments or improvements.

Stand-alone performance support materials exist independently of the software or other environments in which tasks are carried out, but provide employees with information they need to carry out specific tasks. Examples could include:

- A trouble shooting guide that helps service technicians to identify and repair equipment.

- A human resources guide that provides information and advice needed to ensure HR practices comply with applicable laws.

- A guide that helps machine operators set up equipment on the factory floor for optimum working conditions.

These can be contrasted with **embedded** performance support, primarily found in software, in which there is no distinction between an application and the support material. The software interface is designed in such a way that it provides the necessary guidance through work tasks and delivers the appropriate information and advice when, where, and how the employee needs it. With this type of performance support, the designer of the materials works closely together with the software developer. Examples could include:

- A system used by customer support representatives that helps them take and track customer orders. The software supports the process by providing a road map of the key steps, with relevant advice and guidance for each step, and provides assistance with searching for answers to questions commonly asked by customers.

- A production management system to help engineers plan and schedule production. The system structures the planning system, providing background conceptual knowledge on key planning concepts integrated with step-by-step instructions for creating a manufacturing schedule.

Generic support is the same regardless of who you are. It knows nothing about your particular situation and makes no adjustments as a result. Generic support is clearly easier to provide, but is not always going to deliver exactly what you want.

Tailored support is fashioned around your needs. At a relatively simple level this may mean that the support is context-sensitive, i.e. it depends on what you're doing at the time. At a more sophisticated level, the support may take the form of a decision aid or expert system that responds to information that you provide or data that the system has been gathering about you. Perhaps the most tailored support will be human, in the form of a help desk call or a response to a forum posting.

Performance support materials are:

- *at their best when* clear and concise, regularly maintained, well supported by visual media, embedded, tailored;
- *best avoided when* lengthy and laborious, hard to access, inaccurate, poorly laid out.

Mobile learning

The concept of mobile learning, or 'm-learning' is not a new one. For some time now, learning technologists have speculated about the potential for small, hand-held devices to bring learning content to that portion of the workforce that doesn't work behind a desk – the engineers, salespeople, doctors and drivers, the members of the armed and emergency services, and many others. However, until recently, the reality did not match up to the hype; low-powered devices with poor connectivity and very limited memory just weren't capable of delivering on the promise. But a great deal has changed very quickly: PDAs (personal digital assistants) and mobile phones have converged to create powerful smart phones that double as media players, cameras, satellite navigation devices and much more; the memory capacity of mobile devices, whether solid state or magnetic, is growing at such a rate that futurists envisage the day when all the music that has ever been recorded could be stored on a single phone; at the same time 3G (third generation) connectivity has enabled mobile devices to connect with the internet and with an employer's intranet at broadband speeds (with super-speed 4G networks around the corner).

A modern smart phone is as powerful a computer as a desktop PC was just a few years ago. True, the screens are small, but getting larger as touch screens and slide-out keyboards mean that less of the footprint of the device is taken up with buttons. The display is ideal for photos, diagrams, flowcharts, videos, slide shows, animations and limited amounts of text. The input devices are suited to most forms of interactivity, as long as this doesn't involve large amounts of typing.

So, how could mobile devices be used to support learning at the point of need? Possibilities include the use of video to provide demonstrations of tasks, providing instruction with animated slideshows and podcasts, consulting experts using forums and simple mobile telephony, and the use of intelligent troubleshooting guides and decision aids.

Don Taylor describes how just-in-time performance support can make an impact in the most surprising ways. Goalless after 120 minutes of open play, 2009's Carling Cup Final was decided on penalties. Manchester United beat Spurs 4-1, but the real winner was mobile learning, as the Red's goalkeeper Ben Foster revealed afterwards in the Daily Telegraph: "Me and [goalkeeping coach] Eric Steele looked at a little iPod before the penalties were taken. It had a video of their penalty takers. It's a new one for us. When Eric came to the club I'd never seen anything like it before. I don't think any of us had. It's a fantastic tool for us." Minutes later, Foster saved Jamie O'Hara's spot-kick.

Mobile learning is:

- *at its best when* designed for small screens and modest input devices, when accessible in small chunks, when supports offline and online delivery;
- *best avoided when* over-complex, slow, requires too much text input.

Help desks

A help desk is a well-established method for providing performance support on a top-down basis. To avoid the help desk being overwhelmed with queries, it's important that it is not used by employees as their first port of call in the event of difficulty. A good sequence would be:

- Receive training where necessary and available.
- Consult reference materials where these are available.
- If the reference materials don't address your particular problem, check out the FAQs (frequently-asked questions) or past forum postings.

- If your problem hasn't been documented so far, consider posting a query to the forum or, if you must have a fast response, contact the help desk.
- If the help desk can't answer your query, have them put you in touch with the appropriate subject expert.

Help desks can operate by phone, by email, by some form of online instant messaging or via a web form. Typically they will be supported by software which issues 'tickets', prioritises requests, tracks progress and maintains statistics.

A help desk is:

- *at its best when* it is responsive to high priority requests, when backed up by FAQs and other performance support materials, when supported by help desk software, when accessible via a variety of media;
- *best avoided when* slow, poorly organised, used as a first port of call.

Online books

One of the greatest success stories in terms of online learning has been the deployment by content aggregators of large libraries of online books for access by an organisation's employees on a just-in-time basis. Online books are not there to be read from cover to cover; these are authoritative reference works that can provide quick answers to topical problems.

The most successful applications of online books so far have been for IT professionals. Apart from the obvious use of reference sources for troubleshooting, programmers using services such as Books24x7 commonly copy code directly from the books to paste into their applications. Other popular domains include finance, marketing and law.

Online books are:

- *at their best when* highly relevant to the job, are authoritative works, up-to-date, easily searchable;
- *best avoided when* theoretical rather than practical, poorly indexed.

Bottom-up approaches

On-demand learning can also be supported from the bottom-up through the use of technology:

Online search

By far the most popular way to track down information that is not easily available to hand is by using an internet search engine. Facilities such as Google provide a window onto the World Wide Web which most users find quicker and easier to operate than any form of hierarchical menu system or index supplied through a portal (gateway page). This major shift in consumer behaviour has taken place extremely rapidly, but is already deep-rooted. Employees will be very disappointed if they cannot replicate this process when accessing their organisation's data on the intranet.

It's important that the search engine that's used on an organisation's intranet is as similar in scope and power to the familiar internet tools as possible. That means the ability to search documents as well as web pages and to return results in the blink of an eye. Enterprise software, such as knowledge management systems and learning management systems, can be a problem if the main intranet search engine can't see inside; no-one wants to have to use a different search facility for each system if they can avoid it.

Employees may benefit from some guidance in the use of search techniques which will reduce the quantity of items returned and increase their relevance. Content contributors could also be usefully steered to using techniques which help the search engine to index appropriately, including the use of meaningful titles, tags and descriptions.

An intranet search engine is:

- *at its best when* it is as fast as the internet equivalent, it indexes documents as well as web pages, it can search within enterprise systems such as learning management systems or knowledge management systems;
- *best avoided when* slow, covers only a limited body of information.

Using forums

A forum is a simple, asynchronous (self-paced) collaboration tool that has been In used in one form or another and under a variety of names (bulletin boards, discussion forums. message boards) for several decades. A new 'discussion thread' starts when a user of the forum submits a posting, typically a question. Other users can then respond to this posting or extend the discussion on the basis of previous responses. Postings typically take the form of plain text, although some systems allow for more elaborate formatting and the attachment of documents.

Forums can be moderated or un-moderated. When moderated, a nominated individual has to approve each submission before it is posted onto the forum. Moderators also have the power to delete postings or whole threads. Forums are most commonly deployed on web sites or as part of learning management systems. Many systems allow users to 'subscribe' to particular forums or threads, so they can be notified by email when a new posting has been made.

A forum is a powerful tool for on-demand learning. When an employee has a question about some aspect of their work, they can simply start a new thread on the forum and wait for other users to come back with answers. This is unlikely to be the quickest way to obtain a response to a question, but is likely to generate a high quality of reply.

The forum archive also provides a valuable source of answers, because it is quite common for many users to have the same questions. To help users find relevant threads in the archive, it helps if the threads are organised into categories and are searchable.

Forums are:

- *at their best when* experts are monitoring the forum for questions that they can help with, when the threads are categorised and searchable, when users can subscribe in order to obtain updates by email;
- *best avoided when* postings are subject to unnecessary editorial control, when no-one is keeping a look out for new questions arriving.

Using wikis

Wikis are websites for which the content is provided by the website's users, rather than by the owner/publisher. Any wiki user can edit or add to the existing wiki content, making this a truly bottom-up resource. Wiki software provides a simple interface whereby wiki pages cam be edited using either a simple markup language called wikitext or, more commonly now, a WYSIWYG (what you see is what you get) editor along the lines of a simple word processor.

The most popular example of a wiki is the Wikipedia, an online encyclopaedia for which all of the articles have been contributed by enthusiastic volunteers. Although the Wikipedia's users run into hundreds of millions, something like 10,000 people have contributed the content. This is not unusual in web collaboration, where the 90:9:1 rule is said to apply, i.e. for every 100 users, 1 sets up the resource, 9 comment on and refine the resource, and the remaining 90 consume what is produced. Having said that, there are some indications that next generation learners, i.e. those under 30, will be more active in their use of collaborative tools.

There are many varieties of wiki software, some stand-alone packages, some incorporated into more general collaborative tools and virtual learning environments. Because wikis have many uses beyond learning, the decision on whether or how to deploy wikis within the work environment is likely to be made at the enterprise level, with the dominant input coming from the IT department. However, as an I&d professional you still have an important role in affirming the value of wikis for learning and knowledge sharing, and in helping to encourage their use.

Because wikis are so simple in concept and in operation, they make ideal resources for on-demand learning, particularly in the form of online reference guides. A good example of wikis in practice is the Pfizerpedia at biomedical and pharmaceutical company Pfizer. As of November 2008, the application had more than 4500 articles, of which 3,300 had received more than 1000 hits. Since its inception two years previously, there had been more than 10m page views and 79,400 page edits. Nokia uses wikis to coordinate its technical research; IBM has more than 20,000 wikis which it uses for everything from project collaboration to software development; more than half of all employees at investment bank Dresdner Kleinwort are active wiki users. At Janssen-Clag, the whole intranet is now based on a wiki, although they never use the term. They say: "People shouldn't know or care that they are using a wiki. All that matters is that they can easily browse, search and contribute content."

The most common objection to the use of wikis is that, because there is no control over the content, the quality of information will be unreliable. There is, of course, some risk of this, although the quality of content can be monitored and content can be easily 'rolled back' to an earlier, more reliable version. On the whole, though, organisations report few problems with content quality and there is some evidence to believe that the peer review process, which is integral to wikis, leads to higher quality than expert-produced material.

Stewart Mader[76] provides some good advice on how to kick-start the use of wikis: "To successfully grow your wiki into a collaboration and knowledge hub in your organisation, the best way to start is with a grassroots, or bottom-up strategy. To start grassroots adoption, start with a pilot in which a set of groups is given early access to the wiki to start building their collaborative spaces. Along the way, they can be advised and nurtured by a wiki champion to help make it as successful as possible, and this process can be documented to show future benefits of wiki use."

---

[76] *Wikipatterns* by Stewart Mader, Wiley, 2008

Wikis are:

- *at their best when* management places trust in its employees to use wikis responsibly, when the initiative grows from the bottom-up, when new users are provided with templates and guidelines;

- *best avoided when* editorial control is too strict, when they are implemented but not supported.

Conditions for success

On-demand learning occurs whether or not an organisation takes active steps to provide encouragement and support. Every time an employee turns to a colleague for help with a task, they are engaging in on-demand learning. However, on-demand learning is more likely to thrive when l&d professionals recognise that:

- it is often unnecessary, if not completely futile, to try and teach employees everything they need to know to do their jobs; there is too much to know and it changes too quickly;

- resources need to be shifted from teaching everything there is to know, to covering the key underlying concepts, principles and skills formally (unless, of course, the job situation clearly demands that these be memorised / fully embedded) and then providing high quality, context-sensitive, usable, easily-accessible information at the point of need;

- in many organisations it is impossible to provide all necessary information on a top-down basis; employees need to be encouraged and empowered to form communities of practice, to develop knowledge networks, to share best practices, and to collaborate in seeking solutions;

- everyone knows something, nobody knows everything.

Profile: Darren Owen

In this profile, we look at how on-demand learning can be integrated with formal training to provide the basis for a highly-successful software launch.

Hewden Stuart plc is the number one plant hire and equipment rental company in the UK and Europe. The company has approximately 1600 employees geographically dispersed over the UK in 100 branches and one head office in Manchester. Darren Owen started work with the company in 2005 and became involved with Project Horizon, a major enterprise resource planning (ERP) project. He ultimately became the training lead for the launch of the system.

The problem was how to get 1600 employees trained in eight weeks. The audience ranged from those who hadn't been in a classroom for 30 years to some who couldn't wait to get started. A proportion was worried that the new system might mean a cut in jobs. Some were relatively tech-savvy but many did not even know how to turn a PC on. Under the new system, everyone was going to be using a computer and in a very different way to the old DOS-based systems which the company had used previously. As Darren explained, "They needed bringing into the 21st century."

Gently, gently catchy monkey

Darren did consider using e-learning for the formal element of the training, but quickly realised that this was inappropriate for the audience at this point in time. He explains: "Hewden excelled at technical training, in other words pulling a CAT digger apart and repairing it, but getting employees to learn a new computer system – certainly on this scale – was something new. The face-to-face aspect was really important."

Darren also looked at using assessments as part of the course, but the senior leadership in the company felt that this may damage morale. Instead the plan was to give the authority to the trainers to keep an eye on the learners and highlight individuals that may need extra support or training. Most employees attended classroom events, but in some cases the anxiety level at attending a course was so high that they provided 1-2-1 tuition in a small number of cases.

In an effort to make the training as friendly as possible, the classroom sessions were run by the trainees' colleagues rather than by outsiders. These were trained first and went on to become 'super-users' who could provide support when the project went live.

No more door stops

Another important aspect of the project was the support that was provided to employees in terms of on-going reference material. Darren explains: "We could visit any branch and see old training manuals wedging doors open and I just didn't want our manuals ending up being used the same way. ERP implementations are notorious for the volume of change and most of it at the last minute. We also couldn't justify the huge printing and distribution costs for paper based manuals, particularly when they would inevitably change very quickly."

Hewden took what was for them a big leap into the unknown by using LearningGuide as a platform for reference materials to support the roll-out. Employees were introduced to LearningGuide in the classroom, where it was used as the basis for exercises that simulated the real-world environment. It was also here that expectations were clearly set that there were to be no printed guides.

The performance support strategy was to use LearningGuide as the first line of support, followed by support from the trainer and, if all else failed, a call to the help desk. At first the habit was to follow the old familiar route and to ignore the online resource, but that habit has since been reversed. When people rang the help desk, they would send them a link to the LearningGuide. It also helped that *Hirewire*, a new intranet, was set up around the same time by the corporate communications team, and this got employees used to going online for important information. In addition, support material covering the Microsoft Office applications was added to the LearningGuide system, further reinforcing the trend.

The LearningGuide materials used to support the ERP system were developed mainly in-house but with help from a supplier. Darren admits this was a big job, but is sure the effort was worthwhile: "The performance improvements were very visible. We knew whether or not they could follow the new process and work with the new system. In that respect it was pretty black and white compared to some other training programmes."

Darren was born in 1975, obtained a BSc in Computation at UMIST and has since obtained 11 years' consulting experience in the field of technology education, covering government, private and public sectors. Having worked in over 30 countries, Darren has learnt to adapt the style of his training programmes to suit learning styles, personality and cultures. He is now working in Canada on a major global ERP project.

Experiential learning

As learning and development professionals we are most alert to those opportunities which will help employees to 'learn to' carry out some task or fulfil some responsibility; we want to get ahead of the game, to equip employees with the knowledge and skills needed to meet the requirements of current and future job roles. Even when we put in place facilities and resources to support just-in-time learning-on-demand, we still have a forward looking focus, trying to get ahead of the game, even if only at the last minute.

Yet for many people, the greatest insights come not through 'learning to' but by 'learning from' our day-to-day work activities. Experiential learning is literally learning from our experience. It occurs consciously or unconsciously as we reflect upon and react to our own successes and failures at work as well as those of our acquaintances. It introduces an extremely valuable feedback loop into our everyday work:

Doing   Reflecting

Without experiential learning, all we are left with is the 'doing'. We repeat the same actions over and over again, never improving and constantly at risk to every new threat that appears in our environment. Experiential learning is 'doing' plus an essential additional ingredient – reflection. Without reflection, we can have many years of experience and learn less than someone who is a relative newcomer but who has learned how to learn.

The natural way to learn

Experiential learning is the natural way to learn. According to Charles Jennings[77], "70% of adult organisational learning takes place on the job. This learning is gained through experiences that develop, through facing challenges, through solving problems, through special assignments and through other activities that an employee carries out on a day-to-day basis."

We are hard-wired for experiential learning, as John Medina[78] explains: "When we came down from the trees to the savannah, we did not say to ourselves, 'Good lord, give me a book and a lecture so I can spend ten years learning how to survive in this place.' Our survival did not depend upon exposing ourselves to organised, pre-planned packets of information. Our survival depended upon chaotic, reactive information-gathering experiences. That's why one of our best attributes is the ability to learn through a series of increasingly self-corrected ideas."

And what's more, this ability does not fade with age: "The adult brain throughout life retains the ability to change its structure and function in response to experiences."

Employees are well aware of how important experiential learning can be. The National Institute of Adult Continuing Education (NIACE)[79] asked 2076 employees in the UK to identify the activities that had been useful in helping them to do their job better. Here's what came back. The figures show those who found the activity

---

[77] *The Point-of-Need: where effective learning really matters* by Charles Jennings, article in Advance series from Saffron Interactive, 2008
[78] *Brain Rules* by John Medina, Pear Press, 2008
[79] *Practice Makes Perfect* from NIACE, 2007, www.niace.org.uk

'very or quite helpful', with those who found the activity 'of some help' shown in parentheses:

1. Doing your job on a regular basis 82% (13%)

2. Being shown by others how to do certain activities or tasks 62% (23%)

3. Watching and listening to others while they carry out their work 56% (26%)

4. Training courses paid for by your employer or yourself 54% (20%)

5. Reflecting on your performance 53% (30%)

6. Drawing on the skills you picked up while studying for a qualification 45% (21%)

7. Using skills and abilities acquired outside of work 42% (29%)

8. Reading books, manuals and work-related magazines 39% (24%)

9. Using trial and error on the job 38% (27%)

10. Using the internet 29% (18%)

Unfortunately these options are rather ambiguous and overlapping, but it is safe to say that numbers 1, 3, 5 and 9 are all aspects of experiential learning.

The argument for experiential learning

Experiential learning occurs whether we want it to or not, but there are good reasons why we should be actively supporting and encouraging it:

Because everyday work experience is rich with opportunities for learning: However hard you try to create authentic learning scenarios in the classroom, you will never match the real thing.

Because we don't always take the best advantage of these opportunities: In the mad rush of everyday life, we don't always take the time to reflect on what has gone well and what less well. True, if an incident has a major emotional impact on us, we can't help but reflect on it, so much so that we may find it hard to sleep; but there are many less monumental learning opportunities that end up being wasted.

Because, if something goes well, we want to repeat it: Every effect has a corresponding cause, and when these effects are positive, we would be foolish not to try and pinpoint the causes. Obviously we may just have been the beneficiary of good fortune, but chances are there are some good practice lessons to be learned and ideally shared with our colleagues.

Because, if something goes wrong, we want to avoid it happening again: Children soon learn not to bang their head against the wall, because it hurts. But as adults we aren't always so keen to learn from our misfortunes; we often just hope things will work out better next time. It may be more painful to reflect on our failings than our successes, but change is often painful, and learning is change.

According to James Zull[80], "Little true learning takes place from experience alone. There must be a conscious effort to build understanding from the experience, which requires reflection, abstraction and testing the abstractions. Testing our ideas through action is how we find out we are on the right track. The only pathway that seems unproductive for learning is the pathway that excludes testing of ideas."

---

[80] *The art of changing the brain* by James E Zull, Stylus, 2002

Top-down approaches

There are many ways in which an organisation can encourage experiential learning on a top-down basis:

Benchmarking

Benchmarking allows an individual, department or organisation to compare their performance against other, similar entities and against the 'best in class'. In a learning context, benchmarking provides an important opportunity to reflect on performance, not in its absolute sense, but relative to the performance of others. The benchmarking process includes the following stages:

1. Identify those aspects of your work that you want to compare.

2. Identify other entities (individuals, departments, organisations) which also carry out these tasks.

3. Identify those entities that are the leaders in these areas.

4. Compare your performance and practices to the entities you have identified, perhaps through a structured questionnaire or interview.

5. Make a special effort to investigate, perhaps to visit, the best-in-class entities in order to identify their leading-edge practices.

6. Use this information to implement new and improved business practices.

Benchmarking is:

- *at its best when* all parties have something to gain from the experience, when carefully structured, repeated periodically;
- *best avoided when* comparing apples and oranges, when one-sided in terms of the advantage gained, when ad-hoc.

Project reviews

For those whose responsibilities include working on projects, formal project reviews provide a great opportunity for reflective learning. According to Bonnie Collier[81], "They say that the definition of insanity is doing the same thing over again and expecting different results. Those of us who have been at product development a while would agree that sometimes projects feel that way. Why do we keep making the same mistakes over and over? One way to get off this roller coaster is to conduct a project review when your project is over. Try it out. I guarantee that you will never look at a project the same way again."

Michael Greer[82] proposes a two-step approach to the review:

1. "First, prepare and circulate a whole bunch of specific questions about the project and give team members time to think about them and prepare their responses individually.

2. Next, hold a meeting and discuss the team's responses to the questions. The result of this discussion is often a list of lessons learned."

Greer explains that the benefit of the first step, carried out individually by team members, is that "it allows the quieter, more

---

[81] Bonnie Collier, www.projectreview.net
[82] Michael Greer, michaelgreer.biz

analytical people to develop their responses to the questions without being interrupted by the more outgoing, vocal types who might otherwise dominate in the face-to-face meeting."

Project reviews are:

- *at their best when* conducted soon after the completion of the project, when they involve all team members, when the results are acted upon;

- *best avoided when* they are nothing more than a form-filling exercise, when the purpose is to apportion blame.

Action learning

Action learning is a process in which employees work together in small teams, called 'action learning sets', to reflect on their own actions and experiences in order to improve performance. The originator of the concept of action learning is Professor Reginald Revans, based on work he conducted with the Coal Board in the 1940s. He encouraged managers to meet together in small groups, to share their experiences and ask each other questions about what they saw and heard.

Action learning works best when the participants have some responsibility for the introduction of new ways of working or the achievement of complex tasks. For this reason, the approach is a common ingredient in leadership development programmes. The effectiveness of action learning can be measured through the changes that participants make in their work and the practical results of these changes.

To be successful, action learning requires participants to buy-in to the ground rules:

- All set members are equals.
- The discussions must be kept confidential.
- Each participant has a responsibility to learn and to help the development of others.
- Air time must be shared equally.

To help ensure these rules are followed, action learning sets will sometimes be moderated by a facilitator.

In an action set meeting, it is typical for one of the participants to present a current issue. Other participants then ask open questions to help the presenter come to a deeper or different understanding and so be open to new solutions, attitudes and behaviour changes. The participants should not give advice, pass judgement or shift attention to their own situation. The set helps the presenter review their options and decide on action.

Revans' vision for action learning was endorsed by that most contemporary of companies, Google, at the 2007 conference of the Association for Learning Technology. Google's Peter Norvig told the conference that most education should be centred on engaging, real-world projects, and explored in teams. He may not have used the term 'action learning', but that's what he was describing.

Action learning is:

- *at its best when* the participants have the power to act on their conclusions, when the participants are at the same level in the organisation, when the ground rules are adhered to;

- *best avoided when* the focus shifts away from the learning to the task itself, when a vocal minority dominates the meetings.

Job enrichment

With job enrichment you increase the number of tasks that an employee performs, typically by adding more stimulating, varied and challenging elements. The driving force behind the idea of job enrichment was psychologist Frederick Herzberg, who saw the potential for increasing employee motivation. Herzberg[83] described five factors in particular that would make jobs more enjoyable for employees:

1. Skill variety: increasing the number of skills that individuals use while performing work.
2. Task identity: enabling people to perform a job from start to finish.
3. Task significance: providing work that has a direct impact on the organization or its stakeholders.
4. Autonomy: increasing the degree of decision making, and the freedom to choose how and when work is done.
5. Feedback: increasing the amount of recognition for doing a job well, and communicating the results of people's work.

Although Herzberg's prime focus was motivation, clearly job enrichment has the potential for increasing the range of learning opportunities in any particular job.

---

[83] *One More Time: How Do You Motivate Employees?* by Frederick Herzberg, 1968

Job enrichment is:

- *at its best when* you know that the employees in question want this to happen, when operational efficiency is not hampered as a result;
- *best avoided when* the employees are reluctant, when the jobs become too complex or stressful.

Job rotation

Job rotation exposes employees to new learning opportunities by moving them from job to job within the organisation. While this process can be costly to the organisation in terms of disruption and the necessary re-skilling, it gives the employee the opportunity to see how the different jobs fit together and provides the organisation with more flexibility in covering tasks when employees are absent.

Job rotation is not appropriate in every situation. Where specialist skills take many years to develop, it can be harmful to an organisation to see employees move on prematurely and new ones have to start at the bottom of the learning curve. And job rotation can be very unsettling for those employees who are really enjoying what they are doing currently.

In some professions, it can be extremely valuable for the employee to have undertaken a variety of jobs as a prelude to taking on greater responsibility. If an employer denies the employee this opportunity, they will do it for themselves, by changing who they work for.

Job rotation is:

- *at its best when* the employee is enthusiastic about the idea, when the jobs in question provide a variety of new learning opportunities, when the process provides an organisation with valuable cover;

- *best avoided when* the employee is reluctant, when valuable skills will be lost, when the re-training burden is excessive.

Performance appraisals

Performance appraisal, as a routine means for a manager to provide their direct reports with formal feedback on their performance, is a long-established practice in almost all larger organisations. According to the CIPD 2005 survey on performance management[84], 65% of organisations operated a system of individual annual appraisal and 27% a bi-annual scheme.

In concept, appraisals provide organisations and employees with a guarantee: if all else fails, there will be at least one occasion in the year when employees will receive some feedback from their manager and employers will be able to obtain a broad picture of the extent to which performance is meeting expectations. In practice, it seems that some appraisal schemes are failing to achieve even this much – according to research conducted by ACAS, less than half of employees say their manager provides them with feedback on their performance. The view from the HR department seems to depend on the mode of appraisal, as evidenced by these results from the CIPD survey mentioned earlier:

---

[84] Performance management survey report, Chartered Institute of Personnel and Development, September 2005

	Organisations using this feature	Organisations using this feature and believing it to be effective
Individual annual appraisal	65%	83%
Bi-annual appraisal	27%	38%
Rolling appraisal	10%	21%
360-degree appraisal	14%	20%
Peer appraisal	8%	12%
Self appraisal	30%	53%
Subordinate feedback	11%	17%

However imperfect, a formal appraisal process is a necessary ingredient in most organisations' performance management systems. According to appraisal specialists Archer North[85], "The human inclination to judge can create serious motivational, ethical and legal problems in the workplace. Without a structured appraisal system, there is little chance of ensuring that the judgements made will be lawful, fair, defensible and accurate."

Performance appraisals are:

- *at their best when* conducted regularly, when open and honest, when they constitute a two-way discussion;
- *best avoided when* no more than a form-filling exercise, when focused on pay and reward, when they avoid difficult issues.

---

[85] Archer North's *Complete Online Guide to Performance Appraisal* – www.performance-appraisal.com

Continuous improvement

Continuous improvement is a management process whereby business processes are constantly evaluated and improved in terms of their quality, efficiency and flexibility. The emphasis of continuous improvement is on small, incremental steps, rather than quantum leaps.

Some successful implementations of continuous improvement use the approach known as Kaizen (which translates as 'change for the better'). This approach assumes that employees are the best people to identify room for improvement, since they see the processes in action all the time. An organisation that uses this approach has, therefore, to have a culture that encourages and rewards employees for their contribution to the process.

Continuous improvement can operate at an individual level, or through small teams ('Kaizen Groups' or 'Quality Circles').

Continuous improvement can be regarded as an experiential learning strategy because it encourages employees to reflect on the detail of their work, rather than just continuing with the same old practices regardless of their effectiveness.

Continuous improvement is:

- *at its best when* entered into voluntarily, supported by senior management, resulting in change;
- *best avoided when* just another form-filling exercise, not taken seriously by management.

Optimising the working environment

A well-designed working environment can contribute to experiential learning to the extent that it makes it easier to both observe expert performance and to engage in reflective discussions. While peace and quiet is beneficial to those who need to engage in sustained periods of concentration, an environment in which there is little peer-to-peer engagement would not provide sufficient opportunities for reflection. Similarly, if all the beginners are in one place and the more experienced employees in another, there will be inadequate opportunities to learn through observation.

According to Seely Brown and Duquid[86]: "Good office design can produce powerful learning environments. But much of that power comes from experiential learning. People often find what they need to know by virtue of where they sit and who they see rather than by direct communication."

Paul Fairhurst[87], from the Institute for Employment Studies, provides this view of learning and development in 2020:

"The multi-disciplinary give-and-take that characterises innovative problem solving has become accepted practice in the development of high-performance teams. In these communities, learning through active participation, rather than passive knowledge acquisition, is the primary way people master skills and knowledge to become competent team members.

---

[86] *The Social Life of Information* by John Seely Brown and Paul Duquid, Harvard Business School Press, 2002.
[87] *Learning and Development 2020* by Paul Fairhurst, Institute for Employment Studies, September 2008

In terms of the built environment, new office spaces, research facilities and production environments are being designed with many small informal meeting areas, often incorporating a mini-street with coffee bars. This trend follows the example set by British Airways and others in the late 1990s."

Paul goes on to explain how five design factors are fostering informal learning:

- "Eco-diversity: more varied work settings inside and outside the 'office'.

- Spatial transparency: more opportunities for employees to observe the behaviour of each other at work.

- Neutral zones: more deliberate planning, design, and use of spaces not owned by any particular discipline or unit.

- Human scale: smaller scale work areas with less separation from related functional areas.

- Functional inconvenience: designing space to increase the opportunity for chance encounters."

He concludes: "Learning has shifted from training workers to facilitating knowledge acquisition, while an 'always-on' informal learning environment is more responsive to the rapidly changing needs of a networked world."

The working environment is:

- *most conducive for learning when* it facilitates chance encounters, it allows novices to observe experts, it provides neutral spaces in which peers can interact.

- *not conducive for learning when* functional specialists are
  ghettoised, when experts are separated from novices, when
  there are no neutral meeting places.

Bottom-up approaches

Employees can also take the initiative themselves when it comes to
experiential learning and in many cases this happens quite
naturally, as individuals reflect on successes and failures, and talk
things over with colleagues, friends and family. The following are
additional bottom-up initiatives which can be actively facilitated by
employers:

Blogging

A blog is a web log, a personal journal that is made available online
to either users of the internet as a whole or to an organisation's
employees through an intranet. Blog postings are essentially
subjective, one person's perspective on current issues and their
own experiences. Unlike a traditional journal, blogs allow readers
to add their own comments to a posting, allowing for a simple
dialogue to emerge around posts of particular interest.

While there are tens of millions of bloggers on the internet, only a
small proportion maintain their blogs on a regular basis. One
reason for this is that many of the more trivial uses of blogs, to post
photos, links and quick status updates, have migrated to social
networking sites. What's left are enthusiastic writers with
something to say that others find interesting. This includes those
who feel genuinely passionate about a subject and those who use
blogging as a way of boosting their professional profile. A small
minority make money by click-throughs on adverts placed on their
blogs.

For those who are prepared to share their thoughts and experiences with a wider public, there is no doubt that blogging represents an extremely powerful learning tool. Blogging is the very essence of experiential learning, because it encourages, perhaps even compels, the blogger to reflect on their experiences.

Management gurus Seth Godin and Tom Peters[88] discussed how valuable blogging had become to them in a conference discussion available on YouTube. According to Seth, it really doesn't matter if anyone reads the blog; what matters is the metacognition involved in thinking about what you are going to say. You are doing it for yourself to become part of the conversation even if it's very small.

According to Tom, "No single thing in the last 15 years professionally has been more important in my life than blogging. It has changed my life. It has changed my perspective. It has changed my intellectual outlook. It has changed my emotional outlook." And as an extra benefit, blogging is also the "best damn marketing tool by an order of magnitude."

It is relatively easy for an organisation to make blogging possible within the firewall, as there are many stand-alone enterprise blogging tools available and blogging functionality is now routinely included in office collaboration suites. One classic use is for executives to set up blogs as a means for regular communication with employees. Wider usage is likely to be confined to those with specialist perspective to share either with their peers or with users of their services. Blogs can also be used within a blended learning solution as a way for students to maintain and share a learning journal.

---

[88] *Seth Godin & Tom Peters on Blogging*, recording available on YouTube, April 2009

Blogs are:

- *at their best when* voluntary, updated regularly, open and uncensored, they encourage dialogue;

- *best avoided when* they are intended as just more formal employee communication, when overtly self-promotional.

Getting a life

Working life provides a great many valuable learning experiences, but it will never provide the diversity of opportunity that an individual can obtain by maintaining a healthy work-life balance.

Those who overwork are severely damaging their potential to learn, as John Medina points out in *Brain Rules*[89]:

- Exercise boosts brain power.

- People who experience chronic stress are sick more often. If the stress is too severe, or too prolonged, stress begins to harm learning.

- Sleep loss cripples thinking, in just about every way you can measure thinking.

In their article *Cognitive Fitness* for the Harvard Business Review, Gilkey and Kilts[90] make the following recommendations to managers if they are to attain the highest levels of 'cognitive fitness':

- Work hard at play: participate in games and activities, particularly those involving some risk.

---

[89] *Brain Rules* by John Medina, Pear Press, 2008.
[90] *Cognitive Fitness* by Roderick Gilkey and Clint Kilts, Harvard Business Review, November 2007

- Search for patterns: challenge and expand your mind-set by experiencing new places and listening to alternative viewpoints.

- Seek novelty: study a new language, learn to paint, use new technologies, learn a musical instrument.

Above all, what this article recommends is for corporate drones to **get a life**. To be sharp, you need stimulus beyond your office walls. The opportunities for informal learning are severely restricted if your life consists of work, eat and sleep and no more. If your day consists of the same experiences repeated over and over, you're not developing – you're probably not even going to be very good at your job.

Conditions for success

Experiential learning happens whether we plan for it or not, but it will only thrive in a supportive culture. That means:

- a culture that encourages innovation and accepts that mistakes are an inevitable consequence of this;
- a culture that does not seek to apply blame or find scapegoats when initiatives fail;
- a culture in which mistakes from which lessons have been learned are valued as highly as successes;
- a culture that is always looking to learn lessons from the successes and failures of other, comparable organisations;
- a culture in which employees are regularly exposed to new and unfamiliar situations, in order that they can develop and grow;
- a culture in which employees are encouraged to reflect openly on their work experiences;

- a culture that values the participation of all employees in its quest to change and improve;
- a culture that appreciates the importance of diverse out-of-work experiences and encourages a healthy work-life balance.

This culture starts from the top.

Profile: Charles Jennings

Charles Jennings believes firmly in the power of social and experiential learning at work, and has successfully applied these beliefs within the complex and fast-moving environment of an international news agency.

Charles Jennings originally went in to Reuters (now Thomson Reuters), the world's largest international multimedia news agency, in 2001 as a consultant, tasked with drawing up a new learning and development strategy. His client liked the approach and, as in what Charles describes as "every consultant's nightmare", he was asked to come aboard and implement what he had recommended.

Assessing the situation

Charles joined an organisation with a unique profile, employing more than 18,000 people, including 2,500 editorial staff, journalists, photographers and camera operators, and offices in 200 cities in 94 countries. Reuters is the largest provider of content to the internet and supplies data on almost one million shares, bonds and other financial instruments. It updates its financial data at 8,000 times a second (23,000 at peak) and publishes approximately 30,000 headlines and over eight million words every day.

He set about finding out what was currently being spent on l&d. He discovered that when all the hidden costs were taken into account, actual costs were much higher than was previously thought. Charles describes how the regional training operations were run as "fiefdoms, all in competition with each other. There were no standards and massive duplication of effort. Little was shared."

Charles identified six issues which needed attention:

1. The lack of a coherent global learning strategy.
2. A lack of accountability – the supply and demand of learning services were separated organisationally and in budget terms.
3. No ability to gather global management information, including costs.
4. A lack of consistent standards – many different approaches to analysis and design of learning solutions.
5. A drive for volume rather than value – essentially they were running a training fulfilment service. Charles describes this as a 'conspiracy of convenience': performance analysis is not done or done poorly; business managers want 'training'; training managers deliver it; no-one measures it.
6. The lack of a global vendor management strategy, leading to inefficiencies in procurement and inconsistencies in learning outputs.

Charles set up a global learning function, with the aim of developing a common infrastructure – in terms of both structure and systems – and common standards for stakeholder engagement, learning and technology. To steer this new global initiative, Charles took the important step of establishing a company learning governance structure, as embodied by a Learning Advisory Board.

Charles knew that this body needed to be populated primarily by key stakeholders in l&d, not by HR and training people. In spite of its name, this group was not just advisory; it was responsible for decision making. As an example, Charles presented compelling evidence to suggest that moving some aspects of l&d online would not impact on effectiveness. As a result, the group made a clear decision; if the requirement was concerned with knowledge acquisition, then they wouldn't try and meet it in a classroom. As Charles emphasises, "It is better that decisions like these come from stakeholders, not from l&d."

The group set out four key challenges:

1. To build a world-class l&d service more closely aligned with business strategy and priorities.
2. To embed best practice processes in all l&d activities across the company.
3. To provide fast, effective deployment of mission-critical skills and knowledge.
4. To support the business in managing budgets and vendor relationships more efficiently.

One of the first priorities was to push accountability back to the line with functional rather than regional heads and a small central co-ordinating unit. The change in culture was emphasised by changing all job titles from 'training' to 'learning', emphasising the new role as enablers rather than providers.

Learning is a process, not an event

Charles made extensive use of the 70:20:10 model (sometimes referred to as the Princeton University Learning Process) to shape Reuter's learning architecture. This maintains that 70% of learning at work takes place from real-life and on-the-job experiences, 20% through interacting with and observing others and receiving feedback, and 10% from formal training. In other words, a large proportion of learning is experiential in nature, as we are defining it in this book.

Charles acknowledges that these proportions cannot be applied rigidly and that different balances might be needed at different stages in a person's career. He also foresees a shift to something like 45:45:10 if greater use is made of social media within organisations: "Learning is always social. This was at the heart of our approaches at Reuters and our use of learning technologies. Where there is maximum collaboration among learners and where employees can easily capture and publish best practices, then the community as a whole can re-use and leverage its intellectual capital."

The learner is at the heart of this approach, able to access libraries and knowledge bases, communities of practice, experts and coaches, collaborative learning environments, mobile performance support tools and classroom training.

As Charles explains, "We learn through experience, through conversations, through practice and through reflection. These are the criteria by which to assess any design for any learning solution."

Charles Jennings is the Managing Director of Duntroon Associates, a leading learning and performance consultancy company, focused on helping organisations build their ability to deliver maximum business benefit from their workforce. Charles is also a member of The internet Time Alliance, a think-tank of leading practitioners helping organisations 'work smarter' through informal and social learning.

From 2002 until the end of 2008 he was the Chief Learning Officer for Reuters and Thomson Reuters where he had responsibility for developing learning and performance strategy and leading the learning organisation for the firm's 55,000 workforce. He is a leading thinker and practitioner in learning and development, change management, and performance improvement.

His career includes roles as head of the UK national centre for networked learning, as a professor at Southampton Business School, in senior business roles for global companies, and as an evaluator for the European Commission's learning, performance and e-commerce research initiatives. He also sits on steering groups and advisory boards for national and international training and learning bodies

Putting the model to use

Models are fun. In their attempts to explain the complex cause and effect relationships of life, they encourage us to believe that we can become masters of our own destinies. If we're discerning, we'll reflect on the assumptions underlying the model, and test these against our experiences and the experiences of our peers. If the model holds up, it may even provide us with insights, helping to explain why things have happened the way they have in the past, and how they might just turn out in the future, if we were only to make more use of the model as a basis for our decisions.

Having got this far with this book, you may be encouraged by the prospect of becoming a new learning architect yourself (assuming you're not one already). If so then this chapter is for you. It provides some guidelines for ways in which you can put the model to practice in real situations involving real learners. It will also help you to structure your analysis and your decision making, but having said that, there's still plenty of work for you to do. After all, every situation really is different and architects are professionals who are used to thinking for themselves.

The process is described below as a series of steps:

1. Define the population
2. Identify needs
3. Decide what must be tackled formally
4. Decide what can be addressed using non-formal approaches
5. Decide what can be addressed on an on-demand basis
6. Decide how best to support experiential learning
7. Implement and evaluate

Steps 1 and 2 provide an analysis of the situation. Steps 3 to 6 then allow you to shape your learning architecture to meet the business needs and population characteristics that you have identified. In practice, the process is likely to involve many loops and iterations, as you continue to improve your understanding of the situation and to refine your architecture accordingly.

Step 1: Define the population

It's possible to apply the model very generally across a large population, say an organisation's entire workforce, and this may help in making very general policy decisions; but the model will be most useful when applied to a relatively heterogeneous group, whether that's a vertical slice of the organisation (by department, by division, by region) or horizontal (by management level, by level of experience and so on).

You'll know if you've defined the population appropriately if you are then able to make some generalisations about its characteristics. If every characterisation can be summed up as "some are like this, some are like that", then you will have difficulty in coming up with a coherent architecture and would do better to sub-divide the population further.

The following questions will help you to characterise the population. Hopefully, most or all of these questions will be relevant in your case. However, you may need to extend the list to capture the important subtleties of your particular situation:

How much knowledge do the employees concerned already have about the field in which they operate and their particular job responsibilities? The more knowledge they already have, the easier they will find it to add to or modify this in response to changing circumstances. This is because memories do not exist in isolation; they are formed as connections to existing memories. Those with plenty of experience in a particular occupational area will have a solid base on which to build and are likely to have a good idea of what gaps there are in their knowledge. Conversely, novices in a field will have little prior knowledge on which to build and little idea about what gaps there are in this knowledge. They require, and will be grateful for, more structured approaches to learning.

How widely is expertise distributed among the population? When expertise in a particular domain is concentrated in a relatively small group of people, then you will be constrained in your choice of approaches to learning on the basis of simple capacity. You can't expect the same few people to be instructors, coaches, reference sources and champions of good practice when you are also relying on them to use their expertise to fulfil their own, critical job responsibilities. In these circumstances you are more likely to try and capture their expertise in some way that allows for more scalable forms of dissemination.

How fast does this population turn over? In some occupations, the employee population turns over very rapidly, making it even more important than usual to minimise the time it takes to bring new entrants to competence. To make this possible, formal training should ideally concentrate on key skills and core knowledge, leaving less essential information to be delivered on-demand. Another implication of high turnover could be that less emphasis is placed on experiential and developmental learning, although it could be argued that this would make employees less inclined to move on.

How independent are the individuals as learners? Those with good metacognitive skills are better equipped to learn independently. They have a good feel for what they already know, what's missing and how to go about filling the gap. They will benefit from top-down learning but they don't depend on it. For this reason, where resources are tight, efforts are more sensibly directed at those who most need the assistance, i.e. the dependent learners.

How motivated are the employees concerned to learn and develop? Motivated employees are more likely to undertake independent learning activities and to contribute to the learning of those around them. Conversely, those lacking in motivation, perhaps because of poor management or because the job is, for them, no more than a means to an end, will do the minimum required to fulfil their basic job responsibilities and no more.

How much discretion does this population have over the allocation of their time? There are many jobs in which the employees involved have very little choice over the way in which their time is allocated – they are needed to carry out their tasks at specific times if the organisation is to function successfully. These jobs range from the un-skilled to the highly professional, from assembly line workers to soldiers and airline pilots. When an employee's time is rostered, it is unrealistic to expect them to make time for less formal learning activities in the same way as, say, an office-based professional who is working to longer-term objectives. This is not to say that those whose time is rostered cannot engage in a wide range of learning activities, just that these will typically need to be formally added to their list of responsibilities and time specifically allocated for them.

What channels of communication are open to this population?
Many learning interventions depend on the availability of particular communication channels. Some, such as on-job instruction or classroom training, rely on face-to-face contact. Many others need to be mediated in some way, through the telephone or through devices, such as smart phones, PCs and laptops, which connect to an organisation's intranet or the internet. Communication channels are an important enabler for learning, so you'll need to know exactly what channels are available to the population in question and what functionality they are capable of supporting. What devices are provided? What bandwidth can these devices access? What communication tools (web conferencing or social networking for example) are available on the networks in question?

What commonality is there within the population in terms of the tasks performed? It is important to get a feel for the numbers within the population who carry out the same tasks and are therefore likely to share many of the same learning and development needs. It is much easier to justify top-down approaches when the target audience is sizable, particularly when this involves the creation of content.

How important is it to individuals that their learning achievements are formally recognised? In some situations it will be important to employees that their learning be recognised through some formal certification or qualification, particularly when this will have a major influence on their future job prospects either within or beyond the organisation. In these cases, there will undoubtedly be a pressure for more formally-structured interventions.

Step 2: Identify needs

Your next step is to identify the learning and development needs that you wish to address for the population defined in step 1. Ideally these should reflect the established business needs of the organisation and be reflected in clearly-defined statements of competency.

You can be as flexible as you like in defining the scope of your analysis:

- The totality of all the learning and development needs of the target population.
- Just those needs associated with a particular upcoming business change or project.
- Those needs associated with a particular performance problem.
- The development of the target population to take on further responsibilities in the future.

Ask yourself the following questions about each of the major needs that you are required to address:

How critical is it that the employees concerned have the particular knowledge or skill (regardless of how often they may use it)? Critical skills are those that the organisation absolutely depends upon to meet its objectives and its legal responsibilities. In some cases these skills may be used only rarely, such as in an emergency, but that in no way diminishes their importance. When employees are not recruited with the required skills, the organisation has a responsibility to provide this training, typically using a formal intervention with assessed outcomes.

How frequently will the employees concerned need to use the particular knowledge or skill? The Pareto principle applies as well to skills and knowledge as it does to many other aspects of our lives. It is very likely that 20% of the total knowledge and skills required for a particular job are used to fulfil 80% of tasks. The remaining 80% of skills and knowledge will be used more rarely. The implication here is that the learning and development effort is best applied to the most used 20%, whereas the remaining 80% can be covered more superficially and/or provided on an on-demand basis.

How much fluidity of change is there with respect to the associated tasks and goals? Tasks and goals change much more rapidly in some jobs than they do in others, and this is likely to have an impact on the required knowledge and skills. When there is a high degree of fluidity in tasks and goals, it makes less sense to try and provide training on a formal basis and makes more sense to support performance on an on-demand basis.

To what extent will the employees concerned need practical on-job experience in order to acquire the necessary knowledge and skills? Any work-based skill is likely to benefit from practical on-job experience, but in some cases the importance of this experience, relative to formal off-job training, will be much more significant. This will be particularly true when the circumstances in which the job is carried out are hard to simulate in an off-job environment or where the employee is required to exercise judgement in dealing with a very wide range of possible situations. A good example would be the training required to become a doctor or to learn a trade such as plumber or electrician.

How complex is the skill or knowledge required? When a job requires complex skills or knowledge, which for a less-experienced employee would be hard to recall, then there is an argument for supporting any more formal training with on-going support on an on-demand basis.

Would it damage credibility if the employees concerned were to make use of on-demand performance support to support their learning? There are situations in which an organisation's credibility would be damaged if their employees had to consult a reference source before responding to a problem. In these cases, there is no alternative but to make sure the required knowledge and skills are in place before the employee takes up their responsibilities.

Is it vital that the employees concerned are able to carry out their responsibilities smoothly and speedily? Similarly, sometimes there is simply no time available for an employee to consult a reference source before responding to a problem. They have to be able to react quickly on the basis of what they already know. Examples include emergency situations, where immediate action is required, or jobs where the employee has to rapidly carry out a series of transactions, such as on a supermarket checkout. The skills and knowledge needed to carry out these tasks must be acquired up-front before starting the job, with minimal performance support.

Do the tasks involve novel and unpredictable situations? Where it is hard to predict the situations that a job holder will encounter, it becomes impractical to provide very specific up-front training or to develop detailed performance support materials. The employee needs to be provided up-front with the core skills needed to deal with the widest possible variety of situations, but also requires the support of recognised experts on an on-demand basis.

Is it essential that the organisation is able to demonstrate compliance to an external regulator? In many cases, an organisation has to demonstrate to an external regulator or an insurance company that employees have been provided with specific knowledge and skills. Classic examples are in financial services and in situations where there are serious health and safety risks. In these cases, it is important that an organisation can demonstrate that each employee has received the required training and, in many cases, acquired the necessary knowledge and skills. As a result, compliance training is much more likely to be addressed using formal methods.

Step 3: Decide what must be tackled formally

You can now start to shape your solution, starting with those needs that are best addressed, at least in part, through formal learning interventions.

A formal solution is likely to be your most appropriate option when:

- the organisation can only achieve its objectives if the employees in question possess the relevant knowledge and skills;
- the organisation needs to be able to demonstrate compliance to an external regulator;
- a high degree of proficiency is absolutely vital to avoid the chance of an expensive error, damage to the organisation's reputation, or risk to health and safety;
- the employees in question are complete novices and are likely to depend on a structured approach to their initial training;

- the attainment of a formal certification or qualification can make a big difference to the career prospects of the employees in question.

Top-down interventions, such as classroom courses, self-study e-learning, outdoor learning, collaborative distance learning, computer games and simulations, and blended learning, are likely to be the preferred choice in most situations. Bottom-up approaches, such as professional and postgraduate qualifications and formal adult education, are more likely to be used for medium to-long term employee development.

Step 4: Decide what can be addressed using non-formal approaches

Having identified the situations in which a formal approach is necessary, your next task is to decide how non-formal interventions can contribute to meeting the remaining needs in question or to support formal learning.

Non-formal solutions are likely to be appropriate when:

- on-going efforts need to be made to ensure that the skills and knowledge that employees gain through formal training are successfully transferred to effective job performance;
- there is no requirement for the learning in question to be formally assessed;
- on-demand learning is not enough, i.e. when aided performance would damage credibility or when smooth and speedy performance is a priority;
- the employees in question need to be kept up-to-date with on-going developments in their fields of expertise or prepared for a business change;

Top-down approaches to non-formal learning, such as on-job training, coaching, mini-workshops, rapid e-learning, white papers, podcasts, webinars, internal conferences and online video, are likely to be the most appropriate when:

- the knowledge and skills in question are important and/or used regularly;
- the employees in question are less experienced and/or less independent as learners.

Bottom-up approaches to non-formal learning, such as the use of communities of practice, open learning and continuing professional development, will work well when the employees in question:

- have little commonality in terms of their needs;
- are motivated to learn and develop;
- have more job experience;
- are more independent learners;
- have some discretion over the way their time is allocated (or can be allocated time specially to engage in these activities);
- have access to the necessary communication channels, e.g. internet access.

Step 5: Decide what can be addressed on an on-demand basis

Having identified those needs which require a proactive approach, whether formal or non-formal, you can turn your attention to the ways in which you can support performance reactively, on a just-in-time basis. On-demand learning is likely in most cases to act as a support for formal and non-formal learning, but could in some circumstances stand alone.

On-demand learning will be most effective when:

- the task is performed infrequently;
- the task is complex, involves many steps or has many attributes, and is therefore hard to remember;
- the consequence of any error would be intolerable;
- performance depends on knowledge, procedures or approaches that change frequently;
- there is a high turnover of employees and the task is perceived to be simple;
- it is realistic for employees to have the time to consult a reference resource before carrying out the task;
- there is little time or few resources to devote to training.

Top-down approaches to on-demand learning, such as the use of performance support materials, online books, help desks, and mobile learning resources will work best when:

- the knowledge and skills in question are important and/or used regularly;
- expertise is not widely distributed;
- it is important that you control the quality of the support provided;
- the employees in question are less independent as learners.

Bottom-up approaches such as consulting colleagues, online search, using forums and using wikis will work best when the employees in question:

- have little commonality in terms of their needs;
- have more discretion over how they use their time;
- have access to the necessary communication channels;
- are more independent as learners.

Step 6: Decide how best to support experiential learning

You don't have to make a conscious decision to support experiential learning, as it will happen naturally as a matter of course. Having said that, there is much you can do encourage this form of learning through targeted interventions.

Experiential learning will flourish when:

- essential skills and knowledge have already been acquired through other formal and non-formal approaches;
- practical experience is critical to the process of refining and consolidating skills and knowledge;
- employees are motivated to take on greater responsibility or broaden their experience;
- the organisation is committed to a culture of continuous improvement and not of blame.

Top-down approaches such as benchmarking, job rotation, job enrichment, project reviews, performance appraisals, action learning, continuous improvement will all serve to promote and encourage experiential learning. Bottom-up activities, such as personal reflection, reflecting with others, blogging and learning from out-of-work activities, will all flourish in any culture that genuinely supports learning and development.

Step 5: Implement and evaluate

The final step in the process is an obvious one but no less important for that. However well you define your audience and your needs, and however carefully you design your solution, the chances of you getting it right first time are slim. With the design of buildings you have some flexibility to adapt as you move into construction, in response to unforeseen problems and new ideas; with a learning architecture, the process of adaptation is on-going and continuous – you will constantly be finding ways in which your overall strategy can be improved. The creation of a learning architecture is not a project, with a clear end date after which the team can be disbanded; it is an on-going responsibility for the l&d team.

The processes of implementation and evaluation will be enhanced if all major stakeholders are involved throughout. In most cases, that will mean the team that manages your target population and representatives of the population itself. Their input will be invaluable in making sure your strategy is well-targeted, realistic and achievable. They will also be the best placed to measure whether the strategy is bringing the desired results.

Rules are there to be broken

Real life is messy: less like a mechanical device in which every part has its place and behaves predictably most of the time; more like a weather system, the elements of which interact in complex and unpredictable ways, always catching us off our guard. Even the best models can only ever approximate reality and can certainly never be relied upon to replace human judgement. If a model could be created which captured all the vagaries of real-life experience, it would be unusably complex to understand and apply. The model described in this book is no exception: with any luck it will explain many of the situations in which we find ourselves in l&d and help us to predict what will happen if we attempt certain types of interventions with certain types of audiences; but these are only approximations and every situation will be unlike any other.

Perhaps the best rule is to break the rules when you have to, but to do this knowingly. Ignorant people break rules because they don't know that they exist. Stupid people break them when to apply them really would make a positive difference. Astute people break rules because they know that, however well they may apply in other situations, this isn't one of them. They realise that, however well-conceived, no model mirrors reality so well that it is universally applicable.

So, be astute. If you have found the model described in this book helpful then please make use of it as a starting point for your deliberations. Never rely on it as a substitute for intelligent decision-making based on a sound understanding of your unique circumstances.

Profile: Bill Sawyer

In our final profile, we meet Bill Sawyer, who works in curriculum development within the highly-technical and fast-moving environment of Oracle. As you'll see, what might seem at first like a simple case of course-building, actually extends to the provision of a comprehensive technical support service, with major non-formal and on-demand elements.

Bill is currently Senior Manager of Applications Technology Curriculum for Oracle, based in Orlando, Florida. He leads a small team responsible for designing and developing highly-technical training programmes for IT professionals among both Oracle's employees and their customers. The work of Bill's team results in some $12m of course sales for Oracle.

Bill has been working on curriculum development for Oracle for some 15 years, but much has changed in that time. A rapidly-changing technical environment, with less than a year between major software releases, means that design times are highly constrained and that the courses themselves have a short shelf life. As Bill says, "You need to be brutal in decision-making and priority setting."

Instructor-led training

Although it might seem that Bill's work is entirely oriented towards the development of formal courses, he explains that the ratio is actually 2:1 in favour of the informal. Let's take the formal first.

Oracle University delivers instructor-led courses designed by Bill's team. These can be delivered face-to-face, typically in 5-day chunks, as 'Live Virtual Classes', using web conferencing, or sometimes a hybrid of the two, where some students are there in person and some remote. Such long courses might seem a distant memory for many l&d departments but, as Bill says, "These are the folks that have to be trained." The economic constraints suffered by many organisations are not affecting sales of these courses.

The instructor-led elements are supported by Oracle eKits, which replace traditional printed student guides. These are available a week before the course and then afterwards.

Flexible learning materials

Bill's team has started to use an Oracle product called the 'User Productivity Kit', a development environment which simplifies the process of creating course materials, software simulations, assessments and job aids. Customers, particularly end users, are making use of the software simulations for short bursts of highly-focused formal training, as well as for performance support.

The team also produces a wide range of other materials which help IT professionals to develop their knowledge and skills with new software:

- Code examples
- Online labs, which provide a 'sandbox' environment in which developers can test their code
- Comprehensive development guides
- Model implementations, providing examples of what can be achieved with the software and explaining how the results were accomplished

Just-in-time performance support

In the early stages of the development of a new software product, when the software is being modified and rebuilt daily, formal course materials and documentation are simply not available, so a much more responsive approach is required. Bill's team meet the needs of IT professionals at this early stage using a combination of forums and wikis.

The forums allow questions to be answered rapidly and for expertise to be shared. They allow a community to be built around all those people in Oracle who are responsible for getting the product online. The forums provide valuable insights to Bill's team as they start to develop more formal materials which will ultimately be used with Oracle's customers.

The wikis allow documentation to be created at a time when there is no one person with all the answers. The development community as a whole collaborates to make sure that everyone has the best information available at any given point.

Bill's work at Oracle is an exemplar of the ways in which formal, non-formal and on-demand learning can be effectively integrated into an overall strategy which supports the learner at every stage of their journey without ever acting as a brake on what is an exceptionally fast-moving business.

Bill has over 20 years of experience in workplace learning and performance, and is still passionate about the potential for the profession and the learners it helps. Bill's passion extends to his on-going education, as he will soon complete his PhD in Training and Performance Improvement.

Bill has seen every facet of the profession, from being an accomplished instructor, to a well-respected curriculum developer, to the strategic adviser to the President with his previous employer, and the President of the Central Florida ASTD chapter. Bill has extensive experience in International workplace learning and performance. His primary areas of expertise are in technical training, managerial and executive development, and e-learning. He can be reached at Bill@TechnicalTrainer.org or Bill.Sawyer@Oracle.com.

About the author

Clive Shepherd is a consultant specialising in the application of technology to learning and communications in the workplace. With nearly thirty years of experience in this field, Clive is acknowledged as a thought leader in all aspects of e-learning and blended learning.

Clive developed his interest in interactive media at American Express in the early eighties, where he was Director of Training and Creative Services. He went on to co-found Epic, a leading learning content developer, in which he played a variety of management roles.

Since 1997, Clive has helped a wide range of public and private sector organisations to better exploit the potential of online learning and communications. In 2003 he received the Colin Corder Award for services to IT training, and in 2004 the award for

Outstanding Contribution to the Training Industry at the World of Learning conference.

Clive has, for four years, been Chair of the eLearning Network, a not-for-profit organisation supporting the e-learning community. He is also a founding partner in Onlignment, a consultancy specialising in the alignment of online learning and communications to business goals.

Clive contributes regularly to the Onlignment blog and to his personal blog, *Clive on Learning*. He writes a regular column for *e.learning age* and *IT Training* magazines and speaks every year at a wide range of major conferences.

Follow Clive:

Twitter: http://www.twitter.com/cliveshepherd
Clive on Learning: http://clive-shepherd.blogspot.com
LinkedIn: http://uk.linkedin.com/in/cliveshepherd